The Enduring Legacy of
THE DETROIT ATHLETIC CLUB

Driving the Motor City

KEN VOYLES & MARY RODRIQUE

THE History PRESS

Published by The History Press
Charleston, SC 29403
www.historypress.net

DAC logo on cover and images used with permission
of the Detroit Athletic Club.

Cover design by Julie Scofield.

First published 2012

Manufactured in the United States

ISBN 978.1.60949.505.3

Library of Congress Cataloging-in-Publication Data
Voyles, Kenneth H.
The enduring legacy of the Detroit Athletic Club : driving the Motor City / Ken Voyles and Mary Rodrique.
p. cm.
Includes bibliographical references.
ISBN 978-1-60949-505-3
1. Detroit Athletic Club--History. 2. Sports--Michigan--Detroit--History. 3. Detroit (Mich.)--History. 4. Detroit (Mich.)--Social life and customs. 5. Detroit (Mich.)--Biography.
I. Rodrique, Mary. II. Title.
GV584.5.D6V69 2012
796.060774'34--dc23
2012004043

CONTENTS

PREFACE

From its national role in the development of amateur athletics to its involvement in the creation of the American auto industry, the Detroit Athletic Club has been the critical fulcrum for Detroit history. The story of the DAC's long-standing role as a bastion of civic, business, cultural and athletic leadership is a unique tale of modern Detroit. Founded in 1887, the DAC was created by a group of young Detroiters caught up with the amateur athletics movement sweeping the country. Striving to manifest the ideals of competition and brotherhood, they built a center of amateur athletics in Detroit, creating championship teams and individual athletes featuring a wide variety of sports, from baseball and cricket to track and field, from high-wheel cycling to football and, later, basketball.

During these halcyon days, there were never more than four hundred members of the DAC, but all were committed to the spirit of athletics and serving the nation. When the Spanish-American War began, more than twenty-five members volunteered for the Michigan Naval Brigade to help man the auxiliary cruiser USS *Yosemite*.

As the nineteenth century rolled into the twentieth, many members lost interest in amateur sports and focused on business and the growing automobile industry. By late 1912, a group led by automobile advertising man Charlie Hughes was organizing to revitalize the DAC into a modern social organization based in downtown Detroit. The group was led by many synonymous with Detroit: Henry Joy, Hugh Chalmers, Abner Larned, Harry Jewett, Bill Metzger, Frank Navin and Walter Briggs. They hired famed architect Albert Kahn to design a new clubhouse on the present property along Madison Avenue. The magnificent Madison Avenue clubhouse opened to great fanfare in April 1915. So spectacular was its beauty that the official opening became a major event in Detroit history.

By the time of its official opening in 1915, there were just over two thousand members, and the club soon became the city elite's gathering place. With nearly seven hundred members involved in the automobile business, the DAC was dubbed "the Detroit Automobile Club." More than one hundred auto companies and as many auto suppliers were represented by membership; they controlled more than 90 percent of the entire world's automobile production in 1915.

In the ensuing years, the club and its clubhouse have stood the test of time, producing industrial and military leaders during World War I, surviving the Depression and, during World War II, becoming the "general headquarters" of the country's Arsenal of Democracy. Throughout its history, the DAC created its own cigar label, bottled its soft drinks and created a world of culinary delights without equal in Detroit.

Following World War II, the club thrived, as did Detroit and the auto business. But as the city slowly fell on hard times, the DAC lost its appeal and came close to leaving the city. Instead, its members chose to remain committed to Detroit. During this time the club opened its doors to the entire community, creating a diverse membership that helped lead to a resurgence. And as Detroit rebounded in the 1990s, the DAC was on its way to again being one of the best private clubs in the country.

Recognized as one of the top private clubs in the country through the annual Platinum Club awards, the DAC remains home to more than 3,600 members (from Michigan, the United States and the world) in its beautifully restored clubhouse where, in 2015, members will celebrate the building's one hundred years.

Even as Detroit's great institutions have come and gone, the Detroit Athletic Club remains an enduring Motor City institution.

ACKNOWLEDGEMENTS

We would like to thank the DAC Board of Directors and Executive Manager J.G. Ted Gillary for their support of this special project. This publication would not have happened without their willingness to share the amazing story of the Detroit Athletic Club and allowing us to engage in its study.

At the same time, many thanks go to the staff of the award-winning *DAC News* magazine and to the other departments at the club. Thanks also to all the talented *DAC News* freelance writers for well-researched articles produced for the magazine. Some of their material has been reedited for this book. Special thanks to Joseph Cabadas, an automotive historian in his own right, for his work on various DAC stories.

We also want to acknowledge Detroit's many historians but especially Arthur Woodford and Charles Hyde, who have provided valued insights on topics ranging from the Depression's effect on Detroit to the high-flying automotive Dodge brothers.

No thanks would be complete without acknowledging the staffs of the Detroit Public Library's Burton Historical Collection and the National Automotive History Collection, both under the direction of Mark Bowden, for providing a treasure-trove of historic materials on long-ago club members.

A debt of gratitude is extended to the late John Bluth, automotive historian and former editor of the *DAC News*, who was instrumental in first bringing together a thorough history of the club. His groundbreaking efforts truly paved the way for the creation of this in-depth look at the Detroit Athletic Club.

Chapter 1

FOUNDING OF THE DAC

When the new downtown Detroit Athletic Club (DAC) opened in April 1915, the legacy of the dissolved original Woodward Avenue club wasn't so much lost as it was abandoned, generally forgotten and left behind in what had become the piston-driven frenzy of modern Detroit.

Although many of the founders of the "new" DAC were young denizens of that first club, the few tangible memories, artifacts and documents left surrounded its singular success on the amateur athletic fields of late nineteenth-century America. A lack of understanding about that first club may have contributed to the desire for some to distance themselves from the original club and forge a new DAC in a new era of commerce, professional sports and big-city life.

Even a highly respected sportswriter like Eddie Batchelor had the audacity (in 1962) to write, "There was no direct line of succession from the original DAC…to the flourishing downtown organization. The older club had passed out of existence before the new one was formed; the sole link between the two is the name." But statements like that are clearly contrary to the evidence—the efforts of one member to keep the club afloat, the seamless handing over of the name, the connection of many of the founders of the new club to the original club and even the timing. No doubt John Kelsey, who single-handedly kept the original club financially solvent in the final years and was later second president of the new DAC, would dispute such remarks, as would other DAC legends like Henry Joy, Harry Jewett, John Lodge and George Codd, all closely associated with leadership roles in both clubs.

Frank W. Eddy—who, as first president of the DAC, was often called the "father" of the club—George O. Begg and R.E. Raseman were among the twenty-three men who signed the articles of incorporation for the original DAC in April 1887; later, they became charter members of the revitalized club in January 1913. Eddy is, in fact, one of the key names that pops up connected with most of the athletic groups leading up to the creation of the DAC in 1887.

There still is a lack of critical information on the founding of the club (only a handful of documents and photographs exist), and the era of the 1880s and '90s in Detroit remains clouded in mystery, romance and myth. What is clear is that the Detroit Athletic Club was born on the playing fields of Detroit, whether they be cricket, baseball, track and field, football, curling or (of all things) tobogganing. It lived and breathed amateur sports for the next twenty-five years, growing rapidly until the Spanish-American War but then quickly declining as its leaders turned to the automobile industry at the dawn of the twentieth century.

Despite its rapid rise and dramatic fall, it's fair to say that the DAC helped "invent" and promote sports in Detroit, fielding some of the best teams (and individuals) long before the city was dubbed "the city of champions" for its professional teams. Clearly the development of the club was one of the first signs of sports having become a community-wide attraction.

Before the birth of the automobile and before the dawn of professional sports, Detroit was a town on the make. The growth of industry and the power of the machine created a precious new commodity—time—especially for the upper class. This led directly to the pursuit of leisure activities and a new phenomenon known as athletics.

In pre–Civil War Detroit, amateur baseball and cricket teams competed as early as 1857. On October 7, 1858, the *Detroit Free Press* reported the organization of a baseball club with "about 30 gentlemen enrolled" and noted that "the persons comprising the club now forming are gentlemen of respectability and standing."

During the Civil War, young men were collected into the largest gatherings ever seen in the United States. In the Northern armies, hours of boredom were often filled with the playing of baseball, which required little equipment, open space or free time. After the war, soldiers carried home with them the new "national pastime."

In postwar Detroit, many amateur baseball teams sprang into being, playing other teams from the area, the state and the East Coast. While baseball—and, to a declining degree, cricket—was the focal activity for

Detroit's best young men, East Coast interest in amateur track and field events, stimulated and nourished by interest in a rebirth of the Olympic Games, undoubtedly had an impact here.

The various accounts leading to the formation of the original Detroit Athletic Club vary slightly from source to source, but generally, what follows seems to be the best compilation of the disparate sports activities that led to the development of the club.

1857—Peninsula Cricket Club (often called "Peninsular") founded
1878—First mention of "a Detroit Athletic Club," apparently a group from the YMCA
1879—National Association of Amateur Athletics (NAAA) forms
1880s—A "toboggan club" forms in Detroit; sources suggest members of that group and the Peninsula(r) "principally" form DAC
1882—Amateur Athletic Association (AAA) forms
1883—Detroit Amateur Baseball Club forms
1886—Detroit Amateur Athletic Association forms; John Lodge calls "this group" the one that formed the DAC
1887—Detroit Athletic Club formally presents articles of incorporation
1888—Amateur Athletic Union (AAU) forms; DAC at forefront of group that would rule amateur athletics until NCAA domination
1888—DAC Clubhouse is completed
1888—AAU hosts first national track championships at the DAC in September

Obviously, the 1880s saw a burst in amateur athletic competition, and the groups, clubs and organizations began to formalize activities. In an attempt to keep amateur athletics pure of professionalism, a number of the newly formed, mostly East Coast athletic clubs banded together in 1879 to create the National Association of Amateur Athletics (NAAA).

One year earlier, the first public mention of the DAC occurred when an informal group of amateur athletes leased part-time use of the YMCA for exercises and sports instruction. According to YMCA sources, "A group of young executives, sons of their entrepreneur fathers, who 'owned' Detroit, had organized their own teams for baseball in summer, football in the autumn."

This unnamed ad hoc group asked for and was rented its own gym in the YMCA. After a few years, the men decided to form an athletic club of their own. Their remarks when leaving were, "We have had a great time here at the 'Y.'" "We have enjoyed everything, except one item—you won't let us have liquor in our lockers." "We have decided to go up to [Grindley] Field on Woodward near Warren, where there is a little clubhouse."

A new "little organization" formed in 1882, according to the *Detroit News*, and was to have a major impact on the creation of the DAC. It was called the Amateur Athletic Association (AAA), and its apparent sole purpose was to play baseball. It, no doubt, was connected to the national group known as the NAAA; Frank Eddy was one of its originators.

There had been "no such thing in Detroit as the cultivation of general athletic sports until the AAA took hold," wrote *Outing* magazine in 1888. *Outing* was an important national amateur sports publication from 1883 to 1905 and remains a critical source for information about the era in amateur sports.

By 1883, several amateur groups were organizing around Detroit with the express purpose of pursuing success on the baseball field. These included a team that called itself the Detroit Athletic Club Baseball team. When the final DAC took shape, it was reported that ten of the twenty-three original members of the DAC came from that squad. It's possible that this group was actually confused with another 1883 group called the Detroit Amateur Baseball Club. But that same year also saw the emergence of a third new group named the Amateur Athletic Club, according to Batchelor and the *Detroit News*. This group was led by George Bradbeer and George O. Begg, future leaders of the DAC.

Batchelor thought the Amateur Athletic Club had formed to take over what had been known as Peninsular Park, home to the Peninsula(r) Cricket Club. The grounds, owned by Alexander M. Campau, were located between Woodward and Cass, Canfield and Forest and leased for fifty dollars per year. The field was later known as Grindley Field.

The *Detroit News* explained that when the city tried to continue Garfield Avenue across Woodward and through the field, "a clubhouse was erected in one day," effectively stopping the project and leaving the site open for the future DAC to use.

Three years later, in 1886, DAC member John Lodge mentions the formation of the Detroit Amateur Athletic Association (DAAA). The DAAA was possibly just another name for the original AAA formed in 1882. It was most likely this group that Lodge described when he wrote, "In 1887, 13 young men, of whom I was one, met in the old Detroit Light Guard Armory and organized the Detroit Athletic Club, under the leadership of Frank W. Eddy, who would later help found the Amateur Athletic Union." According to Lodge, it was the DAAA that had been renting the grounds on Woodward Avenue from the cricket club.

Outing magazine reported that the "grounds of the old [Detroit] Athletic Association were secured" on a long lease in the "heart of the finest residential portion of the city" for the new Detroit Athletic Club. The six acres were valued at $200,000.

Then, on April 5, 1887, a group of prominent Detroiters, now twenty-three in number, appeared before Wayne County notary public J.V. Gearing (an architect, Gearing was also a founding member) and presented their articles of association, thereby officially launching the DAC. In the preamble of the bylaws, it is stated that the Detroit Athletic Club is to replace the Detroit Amateur Athletic Association.

The twenty-three signers were Frank Eddy, Clarence Black, Walter Ruan, Gerald McMechan, Nate Williams, George Bradbeer, Frederick Joy, George Begg, Frank Preston, H.J. Putnam, Joseph Gearing, Charles Doty, Oren Scotten, Frank Werneken, W.C. Johnson, E.H. Nelson, C.B. Bagby, R.E. Raseman, C.W. Harrah, Henry Lothrop, T. Reed Robert, W.B. Lavelle and E.L. Preston.

The noble goals were stated in the bylaws: "The particular object of the Association shall be to encourage all manly sports and promote physical culture." Clearly, this was a mission statement much broader than the group's baseball foundation, probably reflecting first president Eddy's interest and influence.

At the board meeting of May 10, 1887, held, as many early meetings were, in the offices of the Detroit Stove Works, a committee was formed to investigate possible sites for the DAC and to "make all necessary arrangements in the [current] clubhouse for increasing the accommodations." Lodge later described the habitat of the clubhouse "as compressed and attenuated as the proverbial sardine-tin."

During the June board meeting, several sites were discussed, and it was decided to accept the proposal from Campau for the DAAA grounds that the club was then occupying. That plot of ground had been in the Campau family since 1809, when Barnabas Campau bought four such lots, totaling 30.05 acres. The terms of the ten-year lease called for annual payments of $200.

Wasting no time, the lease was approved and a special meeting called for August 2, 1887, to consider building a new clubhouse. It was decided to issue bonds in the amount of $12,000 to build a new clubhouse to replace several small buildings of which no clear description exists. It was also decided that

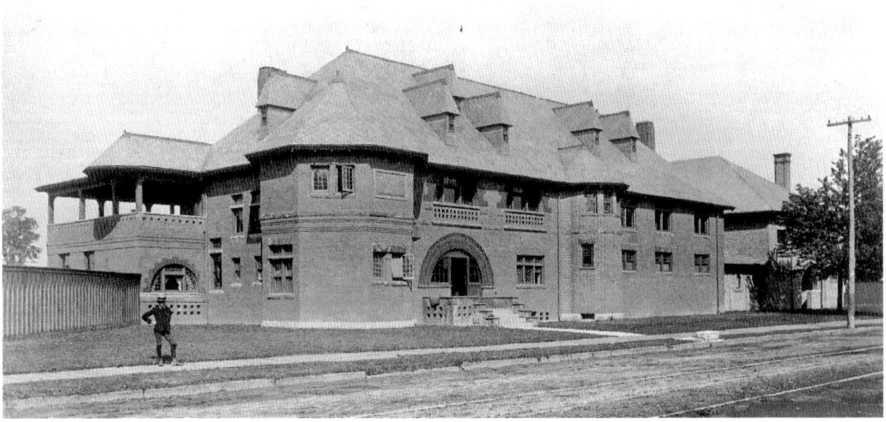

A view of the newly opened Woodward Avenue clubhouse in 1888. *DAC archives.*

no building was to be started until the total amount was subscribed. During the meeting to discuss construction, $1,125 in bonds was sold on the spot. Some preliminary design work had already been done by Gearing since there was a definite price on the proposed construction.

As word about the Detroit Athletic Club spread, interest in the club soared. Many early joiners had prestigious college and athletic backgrounds, marking these men as exceptional in a time when a high school diploma was regarded as a high achievement. The membership was mainly drawn from men between eighteen and twenty-five years of age.

The requirements for membership, not to exceed five hundred, were both liberal and strict. In general, although not stated but understood, the club was for males who were amateur athletes sixteen years and older who, upon the written recommendation of two other members, could apply. The nine-man board of directors would then vote on the applicant. It is noted "that two black balls shall be sufficient to exclude any applicant."

The original dues were in the form of stock certificates valued at ten dollars apiece, each member owning just one share. The strict aspect of membership was that DAC members were not allowed "any participation in competition for pay."

As word spread, other organizations began to take notice of the blooming upstart. The Detroit Curling Club asked permission to build a facility on DAC property and was willing to pay a rental fee of $100 plus taxes; the proposal was turned down. The New York Athletic Club asked to have a DAC representative at an NAAA athletic conference it was to hold.

By September 26, 1887, all the bonds were sold and plans for the new clubhouse had been approved. The first annual meeting, just six months later, in March 1888, was held in the not yet totally finished DAC Clubhouse.

By October, the club had reached 300 members, and the board moved to increase dues to fifteen dollars for the next 50 members and twenty-five dollars after membership reached 350. The twenty-five-dollar shares were sold out by November, and a proposal to sell shares at thirty-five dollars was approved. By December, all the thirty-five-dollar memberships were gone, and a proposal to offer shares at fifty dollars was passed. In just eight months' time, demand for DAC membership pushed the price of shares up 400 percent.

Work on the new clubhouse must have proceeded with breakneck speed through the fall and winter, for on March 13, 1888, the first DAC Annual Meeting was held in the DAC's not yet fully finished new home. So strong was the appeal that by the time of the first annual meeting, 419 members were recorded—a remarkable achievement, considering that the club's official founding took place just eleven months earlier.

Chapter 2
BUILDING AN ATHLETIC IDEAL

Joseph V. Gearing's DAC red brick clubhouse, when completed, dominated the west side of Woodward Avenue between Forest and Canfield Streets, its front door facing Woodward. The new clubhouse was a fairly large structure, 107 feet wide by a maximum of 68 feet deep. Just inside the main entrance was the reception hall, described as finished in hard woods.

The reception hall, in addition to housing an ornamental staircase leading to the second floor, opened, probably to the left, into the director's room, which also served as office of the club and the caretaker's headquarters. Next to that was a reading room furnished with a large table and antique oak chairs. The walls were decorated with drawings of other athletic clubs and early Roman sports; available were athletic magazines, literary journals and local newspapers. There was also a substantial fireplace.

There was a kitchen and accommodations for servants of the club "under the roof in the attic story."

Beyond, and separate from the reading room, were bath and locker rooms with a separate entrance opening directly from the grounds and a separate staircase up to the gymnasium on the second floor. The bathroom featured a then marveled-at twenty- by twelve-foot plunge bath set in the center of the marble paved floor. The pool, which varied in depth from three to five feet, was clad with white enameled bricks and was supplied with a constant flow of city water. Also in the baths were four showers and footbaths and three hundred member lockers.

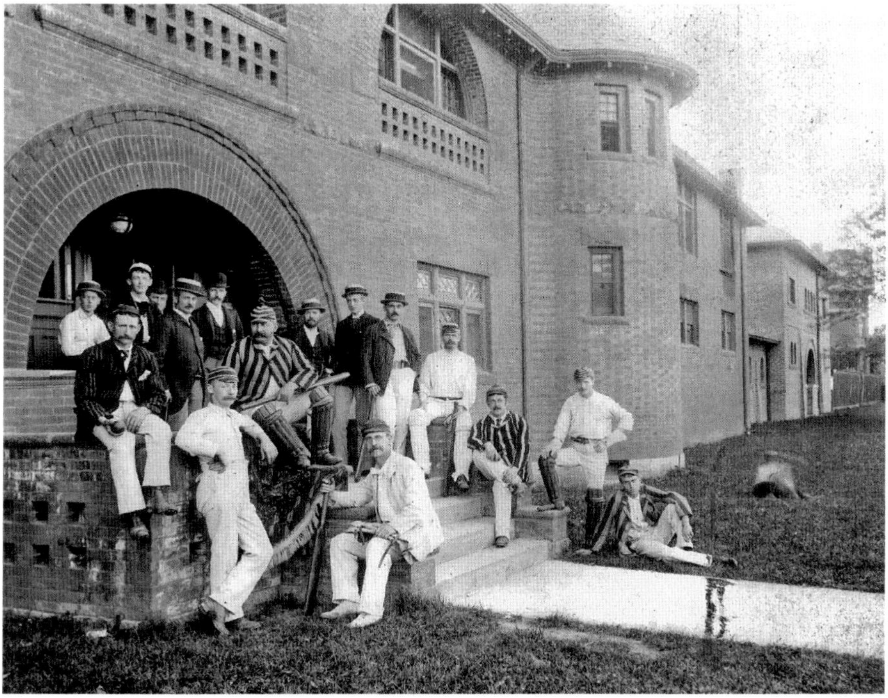

An 1889 DAC cricket team on the front clubhouse steps. *DAC archives.*

The clubhouse had six bowling alleys. The lanes were on the side of the building facing the grounds and "so depressed as to give a clay bottom for the structure." There was a gallery for spectators located behind the deadline, above the level of the alleys.

At the other side of the reception hall, probably to the right, was a billiard parlor equipped with three oak tables and similarly finished chairs. The ground floor also contained a ladies' parlor and toilet room. The whole of the interior was lit by wrought-iron gas fixtures.

The entire upper floor, which measured seventy-five feet by thirty-two feet (and fifteen feet high), was used as a gymnasium. It had a hardwood floor and open-timbered ceiling. The gymnasium was equipped with the latest in exercise devices, ropes and poles for climbing and vaulting equipment horses, parallel and horizontal bars. There were barbells, Indian clubs, boxing gloves and fencing foils.

The lack of basketball hoops highlights the fact that the game was still three years away from being invented. Nevertheless, the DAC gym was undoubtedly the best equipped in the city; it is no wonder that the area's elite sportsmen flocked to the DAC.

There are a few mentions of the clubhouse being used for social affairs, but in a clue to the social nature of the club, there is one interior drawing that depicts a man and a woman walking through the main parlor. Women are also shown in a drawing of the bowling lanes as spectators.

In 1931, an "aged DAC scribe," John Manning, talked about the original club in a *DAC News* article. Besides the sporting events by their nature being social, Manning adds: "I never knew of anybody's paying to see anything at the old DAC except Creatore's Band and the Elks Carnival of 1903, both of which attracted real money to the gate. That last was the outstanding social event of the season."

The bylaws of the DAC offer few clues about social activity but focus on athletics and the governance of the club, which was very similar to today's DAC, with a board of directors and standing committees. There was a Committee on Entertainments listed, which may have organized social events, along with committees for athletics, auditing, gymnasium, billiard and bowling and house and grounds.

The club's outdoor facilities, overlooked by a second-floor balcony that extended over the billiard room on the lower floor, were first class. The quarter-mile running track, designed by the Brooklyn Club's Jack McMaster, was sixteen feet wide except for the south side's finishing stretch and 220-yard straightway, which was twenty feet wide. The whole track was built on a clay base, over which twelve inches of coal cinders (readily available then) had been compacted to form a fast, well-drained running surface.

Within the running track, two baseball diamonds were laid out. Outside the north side of the track were ten tennis courts; six were grass and four were clay. Cricket and football were played inside the track area.

During the summer months, large frames—assembled in the winter for use as a toboggan slide and reaching one-eighth of a mile in length (the club charged admissions for its use)—were stored in the northwest corner of the field. In another corner of the field, probably the southwest, a curling facility was established, likely thanks to some arrangement with the Detroit Curling Club, even though an earlier offer had been turned down. *Outing* noted that the curling group had many members of the DAC.

The whole of the field was bounded by a ten-foot-high wooden fence. Spectators for field events were provided grandstands along the south side of the field near the running track's finish line, with additional seating on a clubhouse balcony situated over the bowling lanes.

By 1887, the original national athletic organization, the NAAA, was failing at its role, and major dissension arose among athletic groups across the country. Detroiter Frank W. Eddy, a zealot regarding amateur athletics, was very active in the formation of a new national group. This group, the Amateur Athletic Union (AAU), took on the NAAA at a national level and soon eclipsed that organization. By 1889, there were nearly ten thousand athletes across the country in AAU clubs, while the NAAA had fallen to fewer than one thousand.

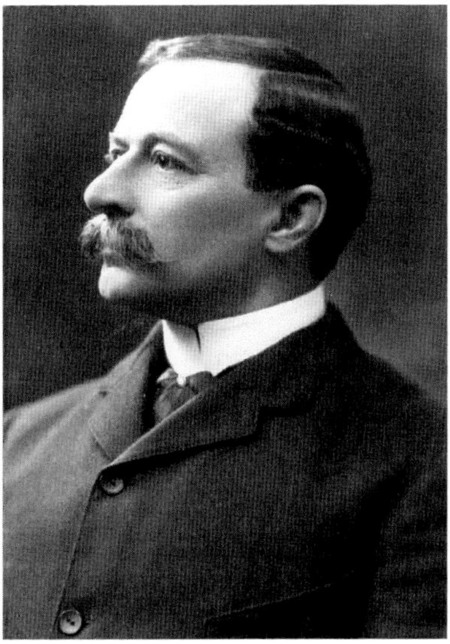

Frank Eddy, "father of the DAC" and founder of the AAU (Amateur Athletic Union). *Burton Historical Collection, Detroit Public Library.*

Outing magazine wrote, "The Union has nationalized athletics, and has proved itself to be national in character. It is composed of more and stronger clubs than the national" and had come to "make itself felt" throughout the United States.

As the DAC Clubhouse was being rushed to completion early in 1888, Club president Eddy, now in his dual role as vice-president of the AAU, must have been busy behind the scenes of the AAU. Through his efforts, the first AAU national field meet was scheduled to be held in Detroit in the new DAC facilities on September 19 of that year. A short mention in the April 24, 1888 board of directors' minutes instructing the club captain and lieutenants to "make arrangements for a field day" are meager instructions for an event that would propel the very new DAC into the highest echelons of amateur sports.

When the great day arrived, everything was ready and the weather cooperated. At 2:00 p.m., when the first events began, the sky was clear and the temperature a comfortable sixty-nine degrees, with a mild wind out of the southwest. According to the *Detroit Free Press*, "Between 5,000 and 6,000 of Detroit's most prominent people honored the occasion with their presence." The *Detroit News* said, "The crowd at 3:30 p.m. was about 9,000 and every up-coming [street]car bringing more."

More than 120 competitors came from East Coast clubs, Chicago and Canada. A front-page column headline in the *Detroit News* proclaimed, "The finest ever held: Verdict of the athletes who competed in Detroit yesterday." P.J. Donohue of the *New York World* newspaper said, "I have covered every athletic meet since 1876 and this was the best I have seen."

According to other reports, the events went off like clockwork, with no delays between them from the time they began until the last of the eighteen trials was over.

In the end, the Manhattan Club won the meet by a wide margin, but at the same time, the nascent Detroit Athletic Club, in one well-managed, glorious afternoon, established itself as a major force in the world of amateur athletics. While the DAC's own athletes did not score many points, the club earned universal accolades for its organization and management of the daylong meet. The positive publicity about the club and its unrivaled facilities helped attract the cream of the area's amateur athletes.

Probably stimulated by the club's notoriety, demand for memberships continued to grow. By December 1888, the DAC's 500th member, Charles T. Rich, was added to the rolls. A meeting was called for March 15, 1889, to amend the articles of association to increase the limit from 500 to 650 members; the amendment passed.

Additionally, recognizing the need for increased facilities to accommodate the rapidly swelling membership, a resolution was approved "authorizing the Board to make such changes in the clubhouse, and to build and furnish such additions not to exceed $5,500." In just one year's time, the DAC had grown so rapidly that it needed expansion.

During the May 17, 1889 board meeting, the House and Grounds Committee reported that contracts for a new gymnasium, designed by J.V. Gearing, had been let for $5,314.

In June 1889, the board agreed to "adopt as a club button" a drawing of a triangle with the letters stacked inside. It is the only record of the creation of the DAC logo; various images of club athletes show just a plain triangle, while others look more like a Greek delta. The DAC would retain use of this delta and the club initials inside a larger square to form the modern emblem.

The new gymnasium and enlarged billiards room were officially opened to the membership on October 1, 1889. There seems to be only one or two pictures of the original clubhouse before the addition. Several were reproduced in *Outing*'s December 1888 issue showing the first DAC Clubhouse just months after it opened and just before its expansion. The expanded clubhouse buildings would remain virtually unchanged until they were abandoned years later.

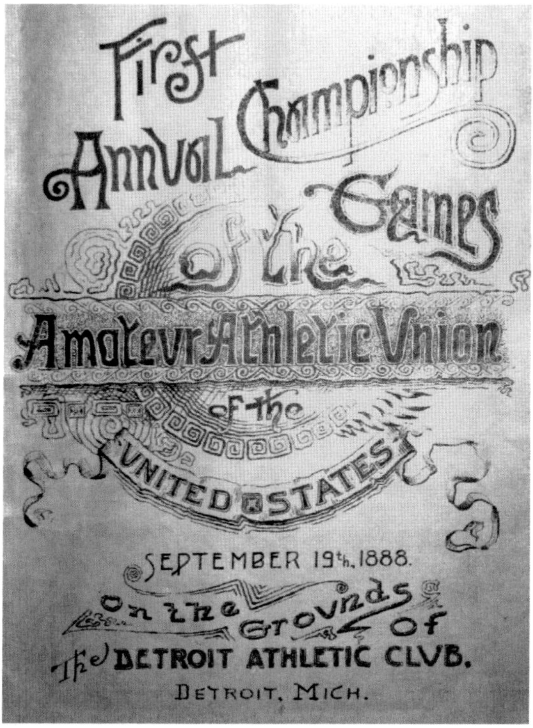

Left: The invitation to the first AAU national event, hosted by the DAC. *Detroit Historical Museum.*

Below: Spectators watch what appears to be a baseball game on the grounds of the DAC. *DAC archives.*

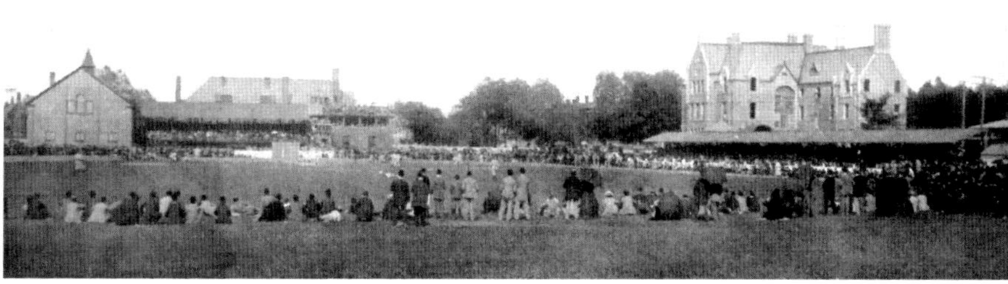

The DAC was three years old before the game of basketball was invented. The original clubhouse gymnasium had no provision for the sport. In 1903, when the club was suffering from declining interest and membership, a complete team of first-rate basketball players, defecting from the Detroit YMCA, arrived on John Kelsey's DAC doorstep. The five, including one of the finest athletes ever produced in Detroit before modern sports, were asking for membership and to represent the club in basketball. Keenly aware of the potential inherent in the new members and the interest in a new DAC sport that they might generate, Kelsey quickly welcomed them.

The DAC five (there were no substitutes) began play in 1904 against any local team they could find and demolished them on arrival. By 1910, the DAC was in a period of steep decline, sustained almost entirely by longtime president Kelsey (no one else wanted the job), and basketball was about the only visible club activity.

The 1911–12 basketball season ended on a positive note with the DAC again beating the YMCA for the city championship. During 1912–13, the basketball team, wearing DAC uniforms and using the DAC name, continued to play even though the old club had virtually ceased to exist.

The basketball team was a later addition to the long-standing sports heritage of the DAC. Its predecessors included national championship baseball teams, national championship track stars and a football squad that would prove to be the first organized grid team inside Detroit's city limits.

Chapter 3

FOUR HORSEMEN LED DAC TO TRACK GLORY

The athletic wave sweeping across America reached Detroit in the spring of 1887, when the new Detroit Athletic Club arose along Woodward Avenue at Canfield. Within its first two years, the club would produce the greatest sprinter of his time, three other national champions and a coach who led track and field athletes to glory in three Olympics.

Long before constant sports programming, before high school and college teams provided mass entertainment, amateur athletics was the only game in town. The DAC made national headlines when it hosted the Amateur Athletic Union's first major track and field day on September 19, 1888. Club president Frank Eddy, a sprinter who seldom missed his daily jog around the cinder track, was instrumental in the formation of the AAU, which governed the sport for over a century.

The fact that the AAU selected the year-old DAC as the venue for its first international contest was a coup. Thousands of spectators came to watch 120 talented athletes compete from clubs and colleges as distant as Cork, Ireland. While the DAC earned praise for managing the competition, its own athletes fared mediocre in the games. That would soon change.

By 1889, DAC co-founder Nate Williams, a graduate of Yale and a former manager of its baseball and football teams, had lured track coach Michael Murphy from his alma mater. Murphy brought the boundless energy and deft skills required to instill a young organization with vigor. Under his tutelage, a number of Detroit's up-and-coming businessmen were transformed into top amateur athletes. Heading the list were the "four horsemen"—John Owen, Harry Jewett, Fred Ducharme and Theodore Luce.

Owen, who came out of nowhere to establish a world record that stood for thirty-one years, offers the most incredible story. John Owen Jr. was born in Detroit on August 18, 1861, the son of a bank president who managed the Detroit Dry Dock Company, a premier shipbuilder. His mother, Jane Cook Owen, inherited a vast family farm that extended north from the Detroit River for miles.

Owen had no formal athletic training. He started to run at age twenty-eight, and his amateur career lasted only two years. But in that span, he won twenty-five 100-yard dashes, ten 220-yard races, two 440-yard contests and claimed a world record in the 100-yard dash as the first man to break ten seconds. Earning national titles in 1889 and 1890, Owen put Michigan on the map for track and field excellence. It was on the wave of his many victories that the DAC thrived. Inspired athletes worked hard and went for other championships.

At the club games in April 1889, sprinters Fred Ducharme, George Jerome, James Duffy and Owen won trials in the 100-yard dash, and Owen took the final in 10⅗ seconds. Soon, Owen had shaved a fraction off that time.

The western AAU championships on June 15, 1889, gave Detroiters the first glimpse of speedy Luther Carey of Chicago, the reigning amateur who beat Owen in the 100-, 220- and 440-yard dashes. Little did Carey know that his records would soon be shattered.

With the arrival of Murphy that June, incredible things started to happen. The coach later recalled first seeing Owen: "He was about five feet, seven inches and only 128 pounds. He had never worn a running shoe and furthermore admitted he was 29. I laughed when they told me this fellow had any speed. But the minute I saw him move over the cinders I knew that I had found a wonder. He had a bounding stride that covered great distance."

In Pittsburgh on June 29, and later in Chatham, Ontario, Owen won sprints. On July 24, he won the Frank Eddy handicap challenge. He actually ran the 100-yard dash in less than ten seconds in August 1889 on the DAC field, but the record was disqualified for a reason lost to history.

Owen's style was to run the first and last twenty yards faster than anyone, but his pace in the middle always was slower. His passion willed him to take running as far as possible. In business, he was much the same. As president of the Cook Farm Company, he conceived the idea for Indian Village, a neighborhood designed by Detroit's leading architects with mansions built along wide, leafy boulevards. It remains one of the city's best districts.

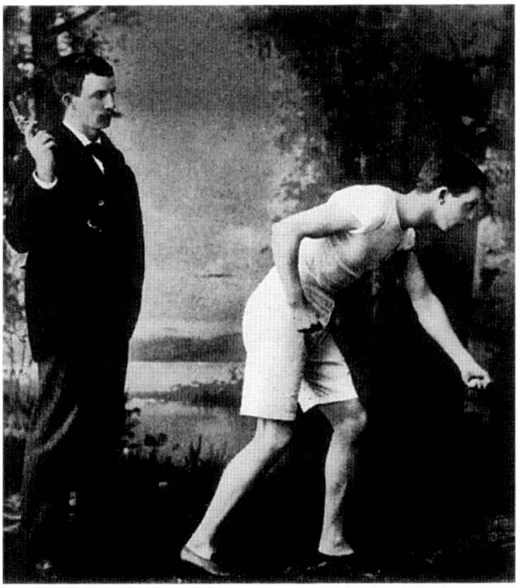

Legendary track coach Mike Murphy and star DAC sprinter John Owen. *DAC archives.*

Murphy was fond of saying that had he trained Owen at age eighteen, he would have put the records for the 100-, 220- and 440-yard dashes where no man would ever touch them again.

At Travers Island, New York, in 1889, Owen won the 100 in 10.4 and the 220 in 23.6 seconds. Charter DAC member John Lodge, in a memoir, recalled how Murphy hoisted Owen on his back and carried him over wet turf that day after all the other sprinters had started across the soggy grass. Murphy intended to place the club's representative on the cinders with clean, bright spikes, which may have been instrumental to his success.

The pinnacle of Owen's racing career occurred on October 11, 1890, on an island in the Potomac River. Owen's historic race took place at the AAU championships on Analostan Island, a pear-shaped mass opposite Georgetown and almost in the shadow of the Washington Monument.

The field had Luther Carey of Princeton, the fastest collegian, and Fred Westing of the New York Athletic Club, the fastest of club sprinters. Also in the finals were two 10.5-second men.

As the starter pistol rang out, Owen got away to a three-foot lead over Carey. Carey nearly made up the lost ground, but Owen regained speed and finished a foot ahead of him. All four timers clocked him at 9.8 seconds.

An Associated Press report said that the crowd went silent. The momentary pause of incredulity was broken by a prolonged burst of applause, and Owen was carried away on his admirers' shoulders. Telegraphs wired the news: "Owen of Detroit has broken the world's record for 100-yards." And he did so from an upright standing start instead of the crouch position that all sprinters later adopted.

Owen's performance was hailed as the most wonderful exhibition of sprinting ever seen in amateur contests. There was no opposition to admitting the time as a record, as it was on a level track later re-measured at one hundred yards and one inch. All other names were erased from the record books, as Owen stood as the premier amateur 100-yard runner of the world.

The greeting he received at home was unprecedented. At least one thousand fans greeted the sprinter at the Michigan Central Depot. The city's first official sports champion was carried from the station to the DAC Clubhouse behind a torchlight procession.

After his world record, Owen, by now a married father and active businessman, decided to retire from racing. Later, he humbly deflected praise by saying that he was lucky or by crediting his wins to Murphy. Owen died in August 1924 after a horseback riding accident at his summer home on Mackinac Island.

His record of 9.8 seconds in the 100-yard dash stood for thirty-one years until Charles Paddock of the Los Angeles Athletic Club ran it in 9.6. The 100-yard dash had given way to the 100-meter competition in most major meets by the 1930s.

The last banner year for DAC athletes was 1892. Harry Jewett, who had been an extraordinary athlete at Notre Dame, won the 100- and 220-yard AAU races for the DAC in New York. Jewett first came to the attention of the DAC at a meet at the University of Michigan. When Murphy, Lodge and others witnessed his amazing skills, he was persistently wooed to join the club. After much cajoling, he finally did. Murphy called him a great all-around athlete, as he equaled all of Owen's records and, in addition, was a good broad and high jumper.

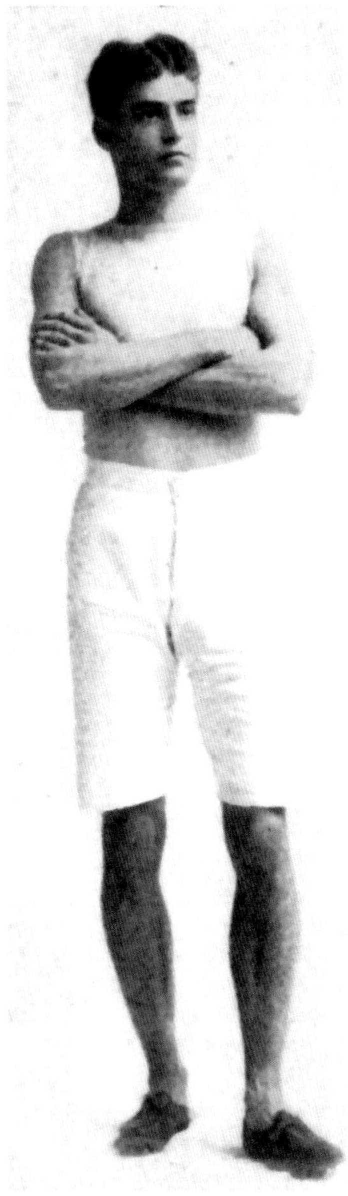

Harry Jewett, a legendary track star and future DAC president. *DAC archives.*

On June 14, 1890, Jewett beat Owen in the 100-yard dash on the DAC grounds in a spectacular upset witnessed by 2,500 spectators. The next day newspaper headlines blared, "King Owen Is Deposed." Jewett was the club's new star.

Like Owen, Jewett excelled in business. He was first a coal dealer and later an auto manufacturer. Jewett won dozens of medals for the DAC, including a national title for the 220-yard dash—the first man to beat twenty-two seconds. In recognition of his wins, the club gave him a gold stopwatch and lifetime membership. He served as club president in 1924. Throughout his career, he invested in land in northern Michigan, and after his death in 1933, his heirs donated over four thousand acres to the state. Jewett's hunting and fishing retreat is now Rifle River State Park.

Fred T. Ducharme, one of three brothers listed among the 1888 DAC members, became a star athlete in the 120- and 220-yard hurdles. Born in Detroit in 1864, Ducharme was a University of Michigan graduate who assisted in the formation of the Ireland & Mathews Manufacturing Company, serving as financial director for thirty-five years. A scion of an old family, Ducharme had membership with the Sons of the American Revolution and the Society of Colonial Wars.

The same day Owen broke the world record, Ducharme scored a national title by setting a record of 16 seconds in high hurdles and established a new record of under 26 seconds for the 220-yard hurdles around a turn. In September 1891, Ducharme won the Canadian championship in 120-yard hurdles in 16⅕ seconds.

Athletic skill ran in the family. Fred's brother Bill was an outstanding baseball player for the two-time national champion DAC Deltas.

Fred Ducharme died in 1944 at his Indian Village residence. He had been a director of Michigan Mutual Liability, the Detroit Bank and a U of M regent.

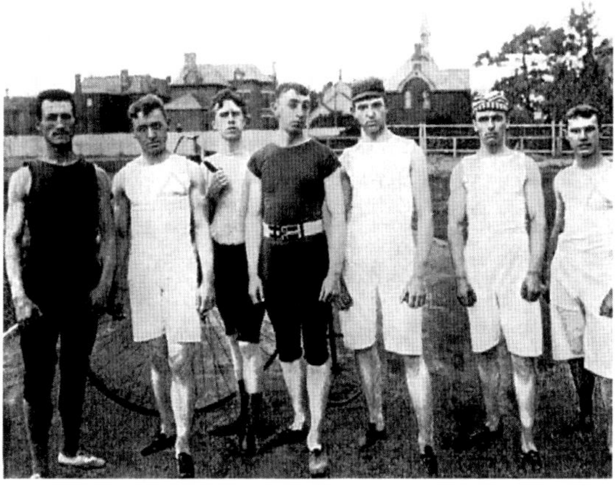

Trainer John Collins (left) with DAC track athletes, including national champion Fred Ducharme (center). *DAC archives.*

The last of the famous "four horsemen," Theodore Luce, began competing as a hurdler but, faced with Ducharme's prowess, moved to pole vault. Luce won his first national title a year after Owen and Ducharme reached their peak.

Born in 1873, Luce was educated in Detroit and started his career with Merchants and Manufacturers Bank in 1890. Later he managed the Detroit office of N.W. Halsey and Company, bankers. He was also vice-president of the Ballantine Company.

In October 1891, at AAU national championships in St. Louis, Luce soared over the bar at ten feet, six and a half inches for a first-place finish and a club record. In 1892, Luce repeated his national triumph by vaulting eleven feet, three-quarters of an inch. Luce's performance may not be considered especially brilliant today, but in 1890, a vault of ten feet was extraordinary. His record of eleven feet, three-quarters of an inch stood for nine years.

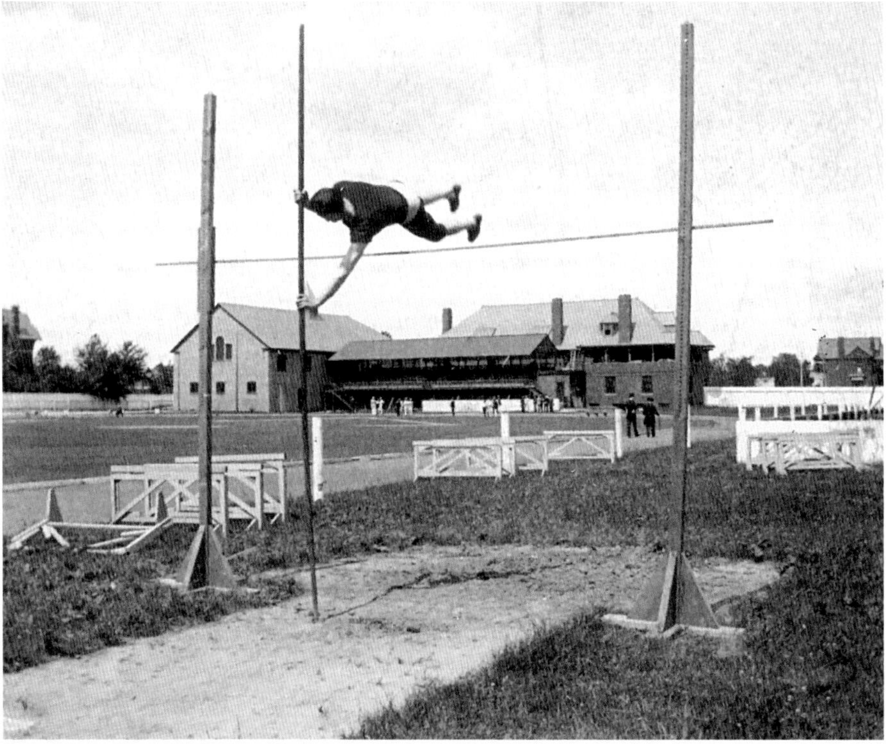

National champion Ted Luce practices vaulting on the DAC grounds (note the clubhouse in the background). *DAC archives.*

The last appearance of the "four horsemen" was at the national championships in New York in 1892. Jewett was carried from his sickbed to win the 100-yard dash in even time, and Luce set a new pole vault record. That year, the DAC team competed in eight open meets and won thirty-six firsts, twenty-seven seconds and twenty-two third places. The club held two world records, three U.S. championships, two Canadian titles and seven Central championships.

Murphy developed several athletes for his DAC track teams. Among them were R.A.Ward, 880-yard dash national champion, 1889; Dennis F. O'Brien, second in pole vault that year; and Charles Dvorak, national pole vault winner in 1901 with a jump of eleven feet, three inches. Dvorak won gold in pole vault in the 1904 Olympics.

Murphy worked with runners W.B. Reidy, Walter Chope and George Codd, who all excelled on the club's amateur baseball squad, too. In 1892, distance runner William Devine won the AAU Western Championship mile race in just under four and a half minutes. A month later, Devine beat a field of international competitors at the Canadian Games in Montreal.

After four years in Detroit, Murphy left to coach University of Pennsylvania athletes and U.S. Olympic teams in 1900, 1908 and 1912. Murphy's athletes won eleven gold, eight silver and four bronze medals in 1900.

A biography from Penn calls Murphy "a legend, well loved by his athletes. Slight of build and deaf, a man of charm and commanding personality, with a remarkable ability to discern talent and train and inspire young men to achieve beyond expectations."

It was Murphy who introduced the crouching start for sprinters. Murphy's departure from the DAC, combined with aging athletes, signaled the end to big-time track competition.

Chapter 4

DAC NINE WERE NATION'S BEST

As the popularity of cricket and rowing began to wane after the Civil War, Americans fell in love with a new national pastime—baseball.

In the late 1880s, before Detroit's professional ball club was called the Tigers, the fledgling Detroit Athletic Club was attracting the city's best amateur ballplayers. Sporting the Greek triangle symbol on their shirts, the DAC Deltas also attracted hundreds of spectators who paid admission to watch the action on the field.

The club nine won the city title and the Western Division championship in 1889, just two years after incorporation. A year later, the Deltas won the coveted national championship and then repeated the feat in 1892. Scheduling problems caused championship series forfeiture in 1891, and the AAU dropped baseball from its sponsorship after 1892, or else the DAC would have likely earned several more national titles.

The DAC nine, however, continued to rule unmatched in its class for years, maintaining a team until 1909. That squad was so good that American League teams signed four players to professional contracts. In 1906, a young man on the verge of one of the greatest professional baseball careers joined the Deltas for several games.

While professional baseball was in its infancy, amateur squads had large public followings, and newspapers across America reported game results on the front page.

The year the DAC was founded, the city's professional ball club (organized in 1881) beat St. Louis for the 1887 world championship. The following year, team owner Frederick Stearns, a drug manufacturer and DAC member, sold most of the players.

Detroit's professional baseball team joined the Western League in 1893. Three years later, the stadium at Michigan and Trumbull was built and would serve as the home of the Tigers for a century.

The Western League became the American League in 1901, and Detroit has played in it ever since. The team was christened the Tigers when players started wearing black-and-orange striped stockings around 1901. Among early fans, the Deltas outdrew the professional Tigers in many seasons.

Dozens of amateur teams provided entertainment on playing fields across the city. Teams from Canada and across the United States played in Detroit. Each summer, the Deltas traveled by railroad to contests around northern Michigan, with a club member fan base in tow.

John Manning reminisced in an early *DAC News* article about trying to crash the spectator section from an alley near the old club's ball field around 1900: "My first visit was marred by a gentleman named Kid Sheers who tore the dickie right out of my new blouse helping me back over the fence. On baseball days the fence was patrolled by bouncers."

The Deltas not only were skilled athletes but were also future business moguls, politicians and civic leaders. John Lodge, a newspaperman and two-term Detroit mayor, played first base and was the team captain and manager. One of the best players was pitcher George P. Codd, who gets a lion's share of credit for the national titles the Deltas took in 1890 and 1892. When first discovered, Codd was still pitching for the University of Michigan varsity team and joined the club nine during summer vacations.

According to his teammates, Codd never wore a fielder's mitt and was a wonderful fielder and a good batter besides being a superb pitcher. Codd was an assistant city attorney and alderman and Detroit mayor in 1905–6. He spent most of his career as a Wayne County Circuit judge and served one term as a Republican congressman for Michigan's First District.

Other players in 1889 were right fielder George Jerome, who also ran track and played football for the DAC; Charles F. Miller, a U of M graduate and Wurlitzer Music Company manager called the best amateur third baseman ever; Charles K. Foster, left fielder and a clerk in Merchants and Manufacturers Bank; and Walter Chope, center and right fielder affiliated with the Michigan Car Company.

Also in the mix were William C. Johnson, second baseman and founder of the Johnson Nelson Company; Walter Walker, an attorney who played catcher; Louis Pelouse, center fielder and a clerk for Smith Jewelry; and right fielder Bill Reidy, son of the manager of the Detroit and Milwaukee Railroad. Reidy drowned in a sailboat accident in 1893.

William H. Ducharme, younger brother of star hurdler Frederick, played first base with the Deltas in 1890. Treasurer of the Kelsey Wheel Company from the time of incorporation, Ducharme was joined by Fred Monahan at second base and William Crowley at shortstop. Another club co-founder who played with the Deltas was Nate Williams, who served as the club's first secretary.

The DAC had a wealth of talented ballplayers, including Ben Guiney, who had a brief stint in the Majors. Guiney, a switch-hitting catcher who played one season with Detroit's first professional club, the National League Wolverines in 1884, joined the Deltas in 1890.

Many others who later went on to become prominent had successful seasons with the DAC ball club. With their roster of city leaders and former professional players, the Deltas often merited several paragraphs of print in the daily newspapers where other amateur clubs might get only a final game score reported.

The Deltas were the cream of the crop and ready to defend their rank as best amateur team in America in 1890. That year, their challengers were a team fielded by the New Jersey Athletic Club. The series to decide the

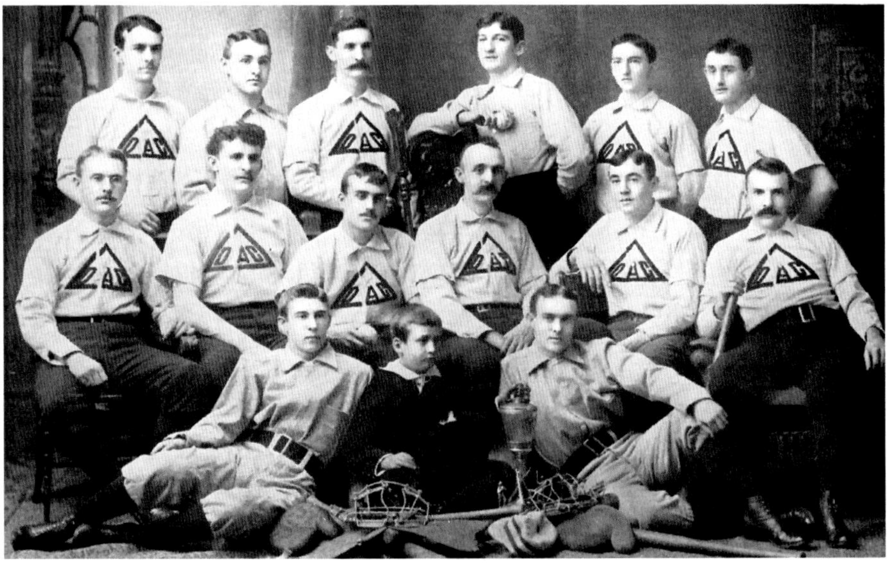

The 1890 national champion DAC baseball team. DAC News *archives*.

AAU title was played on the Polo Grounds in New York. Codd pitched all five games—remarkably the first three on successive days. Three days of rain gave the Deltas' wonder a chance to rest his arm before he won two more contests in a row. A good defense brought the championship to the DAC, as the club batting average for the five games was only a paltry .164. Nonetheless, victory was sweet and represented another national championship for the club to savor.

With the hope of beefing up its hitting, the DAC acquired a number of new players for the 1891 season, including T.E. Robinson, Fred Copeland, Thomas Wilkinson, Hal West, Harry Dingwall, William Frazer and H.J. Erwin. Robert Leadley, former manager of Cleveland's professional team, was manager. The Deltas won the Western Division championship, and the team was scheduled to take on the New Jersey Athletic Club for the national title. But an unfortunate mix-up in dates made it necessary for the DAC to forfeit the series.

The following year, the team added Henry Palmiter, a fine pitcher meant to take some of the pressure off Codd; John Kelsey, another pitcher who could be used as an infielder or outfielder; Frank Bowerman, a catcher who later became a National League star; Joseph Gallagher; and Fred Egan.

Entrepreneur Kelsey played well enough to turn pro but opted to keep baseball a passionate hobby. In 1907, he formed the Kelsey Wheel Company, at one time the sole supplier of wheels to Ford Motor Company. Years later, Kelsey co-owned the Detroit Tigers with fellow DAC members Frank Navin and Walter O. Briggs. All three men served terms as president of the reborn DAC, and Kelsey also kept the old club afloat financially almost single-handedly in its last years.

In 1892, the Deltas easily clinched the Western Division championship over the Cleveland Athletic Club for the third year running and met a team from the YMCA in Washington, D.C., for the title. The series was settled in four games, with the Deltas playing brilliant ball and winning high praise. Today, the DAC proudly displays the silver-plated ornately etched cup that the DAC Deltas won in 1892 for the amateur U.S. championship. It was discovered at an antiques mart in Saline more than one hundred years later.

After the season ended, the AAU abandoned its sponsorship of baseball, so it was no longer possible to stage an official amateur national championship.

Nevertheless, the old club continued to produce strong teams. For a dozen years, beginning in 1894, the Deltas and some of their most ardent fans made a barnstorming weeklong trip across the state to square off against teams in Oscoda, Cheboygan, Petoskey and other cities. Likewise, the

DAC field hosted teams from all over. The Kelsey family archives include newspaper clippings that report on teams from New York to California squaring off against the Deltas on their home turf.

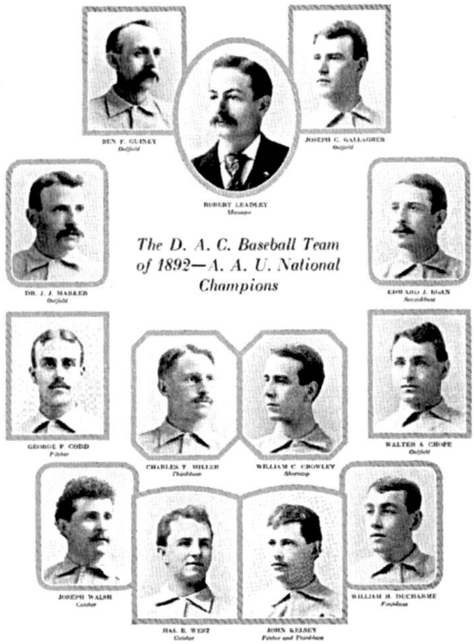

The 1892 national champion DAC Deltas baseball team. DAC News *archives.*

In 1906, a lanky teenage rookie placed on the Tigers disabled list turned up in several Deltas games. He was Tyrus Raymond "Ty" Cobb, on the brink of one of the grandest careers ever in the Major Leagues. Over twenty-four years—twenty-two with the Tigers—Cobb amassed a .367 lifetime batting average, the highest in the history of the game.

The first man inducted into the National Baseball Hall of Fame, Cobb held more than ninety records at retirement. His records for runs scored (2,245) held for over seventy years, and the hits (4,191) records held for almost sixty. Winner of a dozen batting titles and ranked third all time in stolen bases with 892, Cobb no doubt was an asset for the Deltas.

Whatever the injury was that kept him off the Tigers that summer didn't keep the slugger off the DAC playing field. For seven weeks—from mid-July until September 3, when he rejoined the Tigers in St. Louis—Cobb wore the Delta insignia.

In 1909, the final year the original club supported a team, the roster included Fred Blanding, Fred Busch, Jerry Utley and Ernie Vaughn, pitchers; Gerald MacConachie and Ty Denk, catchers; Len Rigley, first base; Frank Gurney, second base; Charles "Chick" Lathers, third base; Scotty Cameron, shortstop; and John Kelsey, Arthur Jones, Bert Lerchen, Heine Liebold and Bobby Hawkins, outfielders. Famed slugger Sam Thompson also played for the Deltas, while Eddie Batchelor managed the team.

Blanding was signed with the Cleveland Indians, for whom he pitched for five seasons. Liebold went to Cleveland and later played for Chicago, Boston and Washington for a fifteen-year Major League career and later became owner of the Indianapolis club of the American Association. Lathers was signed by the Tigers, for whom he played for two seasons before going to the minors. Lerchen spent a couple of years with the Boston Red Sox.

The DAC Deltas, for years giving Detroit the best amateur baseball in the nation, went out at the top of their game.

Chapter 5

DELTAS RENOWNED ON GRIDIRON

A nearly forgotten fact of the original Detroit Athletic Club is that it organized the city's first football team that played any kind of consistent schedule, a schedule that often matched the squad against major college teams and those from other athletic clubs.

For over two decades, from 1887 until 1910, the DAC Deltas were renowned on the gridiron and across the state. That first eleven-man team was formed by Sidney Trowbridge Miller, who went on to a distinguished law career and served on the boards of numerous banks and corporations. Miller had learned the new sport while attending Trinity College in Hartford, Connecticut, and continued playing football at Harvard Law School. After graduation, Miller played Canadian rugby with a team in Windsor, the closest he could come to playing the sport he had learned in college.

The Deltas' heyday in the 1890s and early 1900s was a time when American football resembled the game played on "any given Sunday," but the scoring rules were still evolving. Touchdowns and field goals were worth five points apiece. Athletic clubs and independent teams fielded semi-pro players who made an impact on the sport.

American football evolved from rugby and soccer played at the Ivy League colleges in the East in the 1870s. The evolution into the sport we know today took a major step forward soon after Walter Camp entered Yale in 1876. As he fell during a rugby game against Princeton, Camp threw the ball forward to a teammate, who scored a touchdown. Although

Princeton players complained that the move was illegal, the referee was a Yale undergraduate who ruled the move valid, and Yale went on to win. The forward pass, however, didn't become a legal football move until 1906, and ironically, Camp opposed its inclusion in the game.

Camp was later nicknamed "the father of football," although many others contributed rules as well. When future Packard Motor Car president and DAC co-founder Henry Joy attended Yale in the mid-1880s, he learned the rigors of the game. By then, teams were using the basic T formation, and various scoring rules were being proposed by Camp and accepted by the American Intercollegiate Football Association. These changes included creating a system of downs—allowing one team to stay on offense until the ball touched the ground four times or the team advanced five yards and earned a "first down." The association accepted a Camp proposal to lay down five-yard chalk lines on the field, giving it the appearance of a gridiron, a utensil used to broil meat.

Mixed into the collegiate scene were teams like the DAC and the development of post-collegiate amateur and semi-pro players like young Joy and the founders of the DAC. The Detroit Amateur Athletic Association was organized in 1883, the same year that the University of Michigan Wolverines routed a team called the Detroit Independents organized by U of M alumni.

The Independents played one game against the Wolverines in Ann Arbor, losing 40–5. Today, that event is considered the university's first true intercollegiate football contest on a home field. The Independents could be dubbed the first football team with Detroit in their name, but after the U of M game, the squad abruptly disbanded.

The DAAA group, however, was created by many of the same founders who later formed the larger Detroit Athletic Club. The DAAA rented the grounds of what became the first DAC athletic field, bordering Woodward between Forest and Canfield west to Cass.

When Miller's first team took to the gridiron in 1887, the Wolverines, the first college football team in the Midwest, had only been playing for a few years, and the University of Detroit wouldn't field a team for more than a decade. Among the first DAC footballers were Henry and his brother Richard Joy, Russell Alger, Ben Warren, Walter Brooks and David Carter.

The Deltas launched a seven-game schedule that began with an 18–0 win against Albion College in 1888. Considering themselves strong enough to challenge the Wolverines, the Deltas traveled to Ann Arbor in November 1888. The Deltas held their own, losing 14–6.

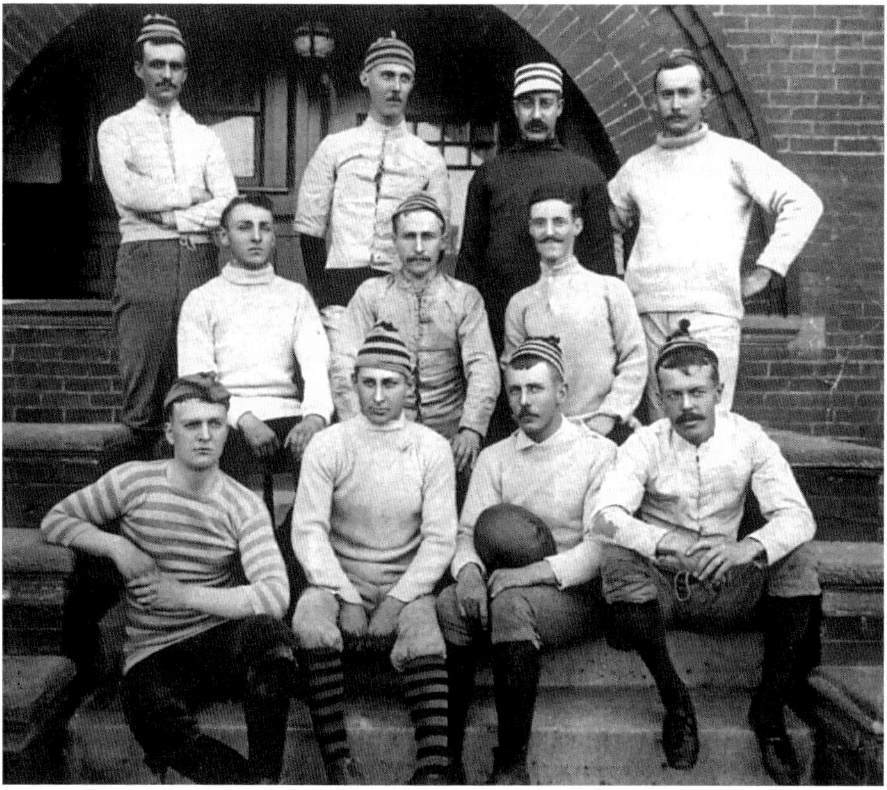

One of the first DAC football teams on the club steps in 1888. *DAC archives.*

Without the benefit of pads, helmets or facemasks, football was a bruising contest, and players typically played just a couple of seasons. Henry Joy gave up the game after 1890 to pursue business interests. Yet before he left, Joy's actions on the field were immortalized in one game played against the University of Pittsburgh alumni on Thanksgiving Day 1889, which both the *Detroit News* and *Detroit Free Press* reported. As snow flurries fell, one of the Pittsburgh players slapped Joy in the face. Joy responded by slugging his opponent in the eye, and the football game quickly devolved into a mêlée on the frozen mud and grass of the DAC athletic field. After the fracas, the referee ejected Joy but not the Pittsburgh player. The fans, mainly from Detroit's leading families, reacted with jeers, forcing the referee to quit the game.

At the conclusion of the feisty contest, played in two forty-five-minute halves, the Deltas won, but the Pittsburgh players left with their heads high, chanting, "Wahoo, wah! Giddy, giddy Pittsburgh. Wahoo, wah!" The gridiron matchup was probably the first-ever Thanksgiving Day game played in Detroit, igniting a tradition later adopted by the Detroit Lions. Meanwhile, the DAC tangled with the Wolverines four more times, getting walloped each time. Still, the university considered the club a worthy opponent, one that could give the varsity players a good workout.

After U of M built its first permanent football field, later called Regents Field, the Wolverines' first home game on October 7, 1893 was against the DAC. The club again held its own but lost 6–0. The fifth and final clash between the teams occurred in 1895, with the DAC taking a major drubbing 42–0, going winless against the Wolverines.

For several years, U of M hosted its big games against Minnesota and Cornell on the DAC field to accommodate the large numbers of Detroit-area alumni.

In addition to colleges, the DAC Deltas faced athletic club teams. By 1894, the Deltas were picking players from the new Detroit High School football team. One of the Deltas players was E.I. "Eddie" Sanderson, a U of M graduate who had played on the varsity team and coached high school football.

U of M football legend Neil Snow was on the club's first board of directors and was certainly an athletic inspiration, although he did not play for the Deltas. Team captain Snow had scored five touchdowns in the first Rose Bowl game in 1902, a rushing record that remains unbroken to this day and is commemorated by a monument in Tournament Park in Pasadena. Snow scored more than half the points (and rushed for a total of 107 yards) in the Wolverines' crushing 49–0 victory over Stanford in that contest—the perfect end to a 9-0 season as rookie coach Fielding Yost's squad racked up a combined score of 550–0 against opponents.

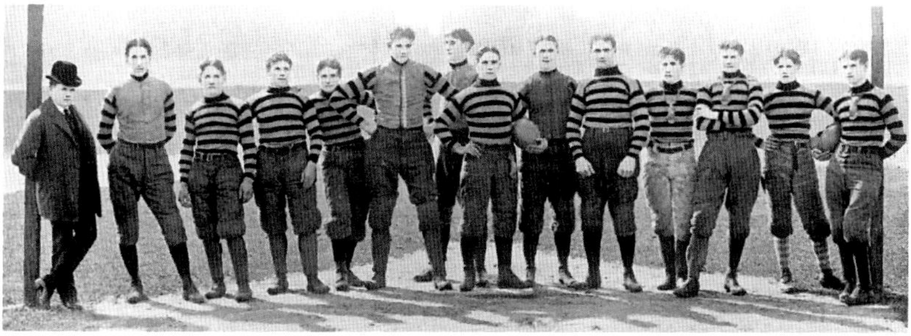

The DAC football team in Indianapolis on Thanksgiving 1897. DAC News *archives.*

A superb all-around athlete, Snow became one of U of M's first two twelve-lettermen after earning letters in football, baseball and track each year. After college, Snow was recruited by the Detroit Tigers, New York Giants and Chicago Cubs but turned them all down, saying that he would never play sports for money.

Snow, who did not play football after college, was considered one of the best coaches and referees in the country, calling games for Yale, Harvard, Princeton, Army and Navy. After a career on the East Coast, Snow joined Detroit Twist Drill Co. in 1909 and eventually became president and general manager.

Although not present at the first recorded meeting of DAC organizers in 1912, Snow became a member of the club's board of directors at its charter-signing meeting on January 4, 1913. A little over a year later, with groundbreaking for the Madison Avenue clubhouse still months away, Snow sought medical attention after feeling ill following a strenuous workout at the Detroit Racket Club. He collapsed on the floor of his doctor's office and died of heart failure, which some blamed on an "athletic heart" condition, according to his obituary published in January 1914.

By the time of Snow's death, many of the amateur athletes who had excelled on the original DAC's playing fields were settling down to raise families and were involved with the growing automotive field. Some of the football stars of that early club were 1899 team manager C. David Widman, who later served as club president, and his brothers George, one of the best halfbacks the club ever knew, and Chuck, who inspired the creation of the U of M fight song. Halfback Chuck Widman had made a long run for the Wolverines in a game against Chicago in 1898, clinching a "champions of the West" title for U of M and inspiring the famous marching song "Hail to the Victors."

Other Deltas of the gridiron were fullback Edwin Smith, quarterback John Finlayson and halfbacks Jimmy Campbell and Ray Cooper.

As the Deltas reached their zenith around 1907, they compiled a winning record (4-3-1) against Michigan State Agricultural College while also winning a city championship. The team's decline came abruptly, and it ceased play after the 1910 season.

Chapter 6

MEMBERS EMBRACE THE SPORTING LIFE

While baseball and track stars of the club got their due as national champions, the earliest DAC members were involved in a host of other sports, including bowling, billiards, boxing, cricket, cycling and golf. Bowling was popular enough to merit a center in the original Woodward Avenue clubhouse—probably the most expensive sporting equipment installed and a clear indication of members' interest.

The American Bowling Congress was founded in 1895, regulating lane size and other rules and staging its first national competition in Chicago on January 8, 1902. There are no available records of early DAC bowling except for a portrait of the DAC city championship team of 1889, which is displayed in the hallway leading to the Abbey bowling center.

Three-man committees presided over billiards and bowling. The clubhouse had an oak-finished billiards room with three ornately carved tables. The bowling center, contained in a side wing, housed six lanes with a spectator gallery.

Four of the five 1889 DAC champion bowlers were profiled in the *1908 Book of Detroiters*. They were George Begg, president of Champion Lumber; George Bradbeer, president of the Wayne Belting Co.; Emory Clark, president of the First National Bank; and Richard Raseman, a prominent architect. William Craig, a Deltas football player and track runner, completed the lineup.

In an early *DAC News* "Spilling the Pins" column, members were encouraged to bowl regardless of skill level. That "just come out and have

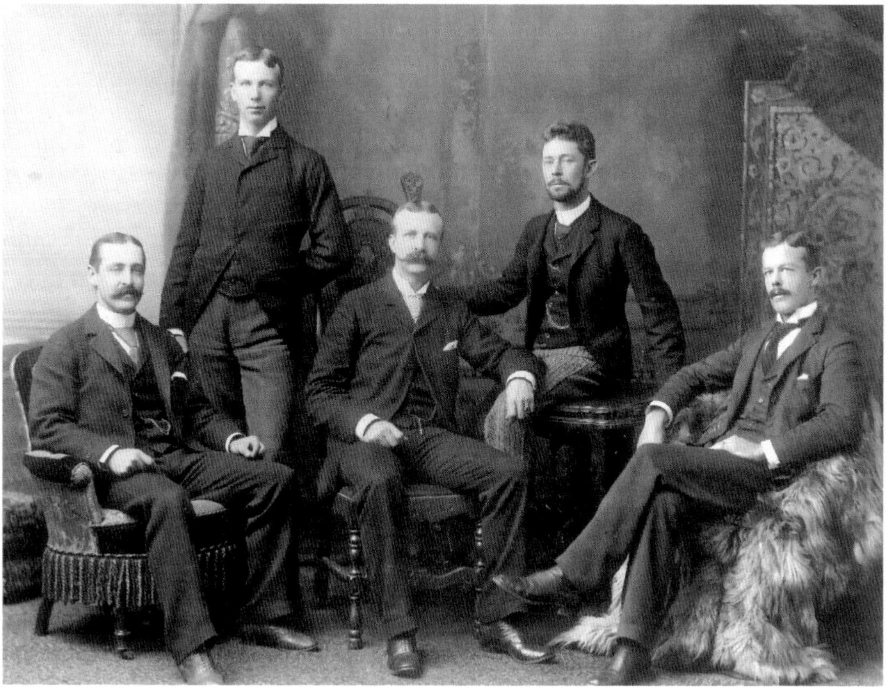

The 1889 amateur champion DAC bowlers. *DAC archives.*

fun" attitude is probably why bowling has remained integral to the DAC through its history.

When the DAC opened in 1887, its physical director was former Michigan boxing champion John Collins, once considered a strong contender for the American lightweight title, having beaten Canadian national champion Harry Gilmore twice. Born in England, Collins came to the United States at age three. He gained prominence locally as a boxer in his early teens. Hardly a moneymaking venture then, he opted for a career as a physical director. At the DAC, he coached all sports and reportedly didn't care much for boxing, but the club hosted lively sparring exhibitions that received press coverage. One 1889 news report described an evening of wrestling and boxing with live music. Collins took part in the boxing exhibition.

Despite his background, Collins only trained one boxer, Tommy Burns, who became Detroit's first heavyweight champion. Burns came to Michigan from Canada, and by his late teens, he was broad shouldered, barrel-chested and living in Detroit.

Burns's first fight was in 1900 quite by accident. He had gone to Delray to watch Fred Thornton fight. But when Thornton's opponent didn't show, the nineteen-year-old Burns was offered a small sum to stand in and cleaned Thornton's clock in five rounds. Over the next four years, he fought twenty-seven matches, mostly in Detroit and Delray, then a village on Detroit's industrial waterfront and now part of the city. Burns won twenty-three fights, with eighteen knockouts, and fought three three-round exhibitions at the DAC in 1902. Although prize fighting was illegal, regulated sparring contests were common.

In December 1902, Burns knocked out Tom McCune in seven rounds in Detroit for the Michigan state middleweight title. Heavyweight champ Jim Jeffries retired in 1906, and Burns claimed his title by defeating another top contender. Burns held the title until December 1908, when he faced Jack Johnson, the first African American boxing champion. The two squared off in Australia, and Burns got knocked out in a lopsided fourteen-round fight.

Burns eventually parted with the DAC, and Collins left the club in 1902 for Central High School, now Wayne State University's Old Main. Collins directed all sports there and established a reputation as an excellent coach and mentor.

While Americans were becoming enamored with baseball around this time, the athletes of the DAC had a brief fling with the national sport of England: cricket. Squads from the DAC and earlier organizations engaged in cricket from the mid-1850s to the early 1900s.

Few records exist of the games played by the DAC or the earlier Peninsula Cricket Club, but the team was known enough for the "Australian 8th Eleven" to visit Detroit in October 1893 while on a nationwide tour. The Aussies prevailed in the local two-day match by "an inning and 157 runs."

British-born Robert Ridgley and Charles Calvert Jr. played cricket first for the Peninsula Club and then the DAC. One of their teammates was George Codd, who, after an 1881 match, witnessed his first baseball game on an adjoining field. The future judge was instantly smitten. He became a great pitcher at the University of Michigan and the DAC Deltas' two-time national championship baseball teams. Still, Codd continued as a bowler for DAC cricket teams.

British transplant and prominent Detroit architect H.J. Maxwell Grylls played cricket with the DAC team and is immortalized in a portrait of athletes snapped on the clubhouse front porch. He was a co-founder of architectural firm Smith, Hinchman and Grylls, which exists today as the Smith Group.

Playing tennis in summer and tobogganing in winter at the DAC, club member Dudley Smith also served on the managing committee of the Peninsula Cricket Club. Smith was president of T.B. Rayl Co., a hardware concern, and was a writer and avid sportsman who liked archery, bowling and golf.

One of the best batsmen of the old Peninsula Club, Fred Bamford, was named captain of the DAC cricket team in the late 1880s. He was a devotee of curling and lawn bowling.

The DAC cricketers played opponents from several Canadian cities, including Hamilton, London and Guelph, as well as Chicago. The high point for cricket in Detroit seems to have been the formation of the Inter City Cricket League in 1891. While the sport flourished in other places,

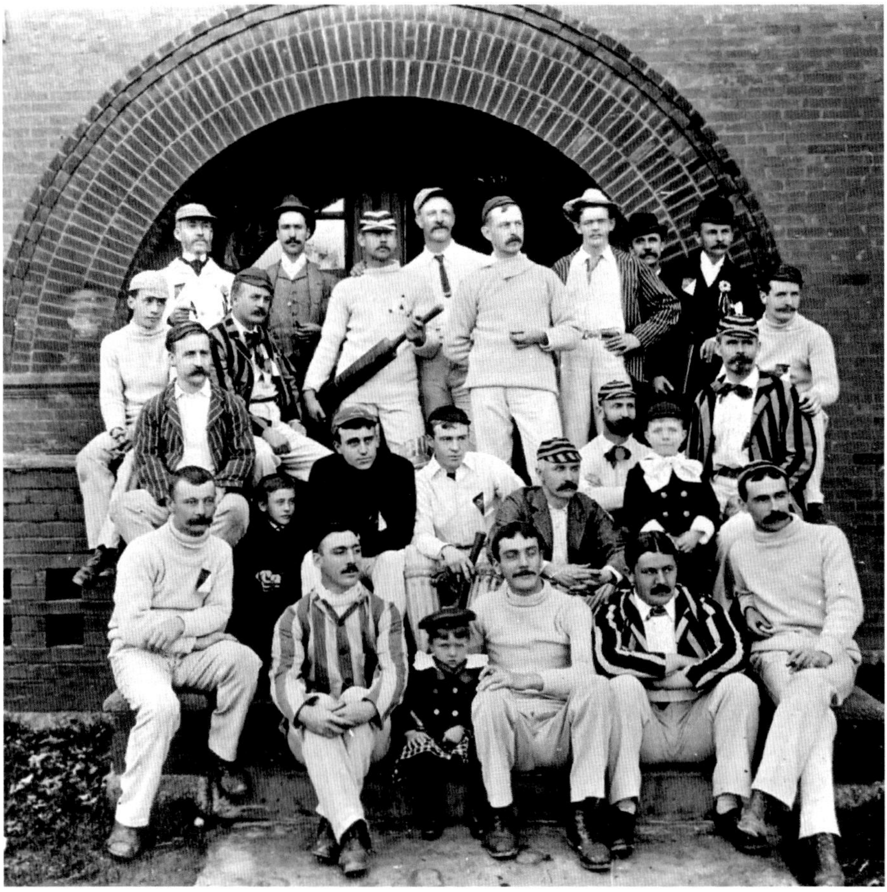

Another early club cricket squad by the front door. *DAC archives.*

it was less popular in Detroit. While cricket fields require a fair amount of preparation, baseball can be played on any grass or sandlot, probably one of the reasons for baseball's ultimate rise in popularity.

The DAC cricket team folded about 1908. Bamford was captain in 1888 when the Peninsulars were absorbed by the DAC, and he remained in that position about twenty years.

As baseball swept the country, it was rivaled in popularity only by the solitary pursuit of bicycling. In Detroit, cycling was incredibly popular, with 80 percent of residents pedaling for transportation and exercise. The DAC athletic fields had a cycling track, and the club hosted races and long tours throughout the countryside.

A program from an 1893 DAC field day lists three races: a quarter-mile bicycle race, a one-mile contest and a half-mile "boys" competition. Serving as judges were some DAC top athletes, including Fred Ducharme, Ted Luce, Harry Jewett and George Codd.

Bike racer George Grant, who later joined the DAC, set the world record for the twenty-five-mile race on Belle Isle. Grant and his brother Charles would later organize the first Detroit Auto Show and form their own automobile company, producing the Grant automobile.

Brothers and high-profile club members Horace and John Dodge also made the transition from bicycle to automobile. Both were involved with the Detroit Wheelmen and participated in bicycle races on Belle Isle. The Dodge brothers manufactured bicycles until 1901.

The club's 1921–22 president, William Metzger, served as the first president of the Detroit Wheelmen. Metzger sold bikes, including the penny-farthing high-wheel model, from his Detroit shop on Grand River.

Other DAC bike enthusiasts were Fred Case, who served as treasurer of the Wheelmen during Metzger's tenure, and A.F. Peck, of the wholesale paper firm Beecher, Peck and Lewis, who organized bicycle exhibits for the Wheelmen. Exhibits typically involved several races on a one-mile track, with some of the fastest amateurs in America competing for prizes.

The Wheelmen, with headquarters on Washington Boulevard near Grand Circus Park, were one of the largest bicycle clubs affiliated with the League of American Wheelmen and hosted the organization's national convention in 1891. Thousands of bicyclists paraded through town, and races were staged during the convention. The Wheelmen later became known as the League of American Bicyclists.

Not just a social group, the Wheelmen lobbied for better roads. Muddy and impassable streets made bicycling difficult, and rotted cedar block pavement

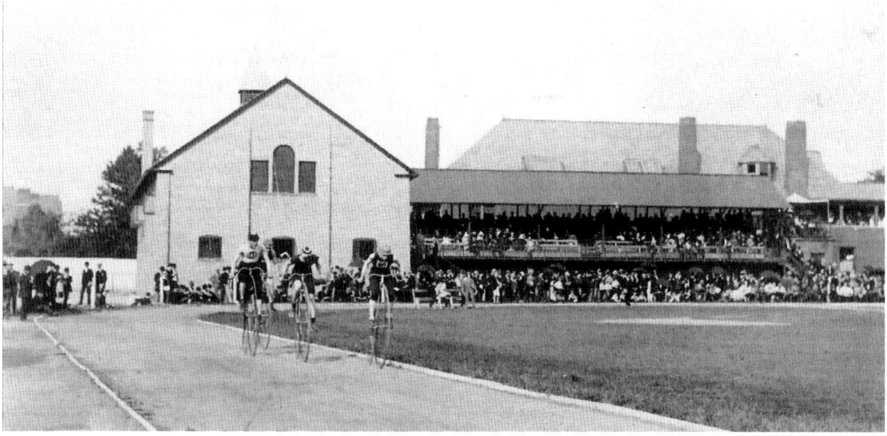

A high-wheel bicycle race at the DAC in 1893. *DAC archives.*

created dangerous potholes. Bicyclists were campaigning for good roads a decade before the creation of the Automobile Association of America.

The best-known cyclist of his day was the DAC's Eddie Bald, dubbed "Cannonball" Bald, who pedaled to glory on tracks across the Midwest. His fame was such that an 1897 piece of sheet music, "The White Flyer Two-Step," was dedicated in his honor. In 1898, Bald participated in one of the infamous six-day bicycle races at Madison Square Garden, one of the last events of its kind before New York banned such endurance contests.

Bicycling not only launched the good roads movement, but the advanced techniques used to assemble millions of bicycles were readily adaptable to automobile production as well. Even the vast network of bicycle repair shops evolved into the nation's first gas stations.

Although the DAC has never had a home golf course, club members are avid golfers who have founded, managed and promoted golf courses to sate their passion. Perhaps the most renowned is the storied Oakland Hills, which has hosted U.S. Opens, PGA championships, U.S. Senior opens and the prestigious Ryder Cup. It was founded by charter DAC members Joseph Mack and Norval Hawkins in October 1916.

Eminent Scottish golf course architect Donald Ross designed Oakland Hills, and Walter Hagen, fresh from winning the 1918 Open at Pinehurst, was secured as the first pro and took up residence in the DAC Clubhouse.

From the earliest days of the club, members enjoyed a wide range of robust athletic pursuits.

Chapter 7

YOSEMITE CRUISES INTO NAVAL HISTORY

They were the cream of Detroit society—University of Michigan students and faculty, gifted athletes from the Detroit Athletic Club and privileged members of the elite Detroit Club. They helped form what became known as the "millionaires' navy" that went off to fight the "Splendid Little War" against Spain in the summer of 1898.

The crew of the auxiliary cruiser USS *Yosemite* included two future American secretaries of the navy, a pair of the DAC's most famous athletes and future industrial giants, a humble "landsman" who would later join the DAC and write a book about the crew's experiences, several sets of brothers, one father-and-son pair and a future Olympic rower who was also the son of a well-known general. All told, thirteen members of the DAC served abroad the famed vessel; seven would remain members when the DAC moved to its new clubhouse on Madison Avenue. Another twenty-nine young sailors from the *Yosemite* would join the new club in 1915. When the United States entered World War I, ten of these men would answer the call to military service.

The *Yosemite* experience remains a unique one in the annals of our nation's military history. During its tour of combat duty, the *Yosemite* crew participated in the initial invasion of Cuba, became embroiled in a minor controversy and gained fame for single-handedly battling a small Spanish fleet while blockading Puerto Rico's San Juan Harbor.

Five years before the conflict with Spain, Michigan formed the Michigan Naval Brigade (also known as the naval reserves or militia). The men who formed the core of the brigade, which operated out of armories in Detroit and other Michigan cities, were highly educated. Nearly 75 percent of the 18 officers and 270 sailors who made up the *Yosemite* crew were university graduates (including an entire engineering class and the engineering dean from U of M).

The unit came about largely through the efforts of Truman H. Newberry, a member of the DAC and a future secretary of the U.S. Navy. Newberry and Cyrus Lathrop were able to secure some funding for the reserves, which mainly had to support themselves.

When the "Splendid Little War" began and President McKinley called for volunteers, the reserves were among the first to muster. In a ceremony one historian called "a brilliant patriotic gesture," the crew was sworn in aboard the gunboat USS *Yantic* anchored in the Detroit River off Bates Street.

In his book *City of Destiny*, historian George Stark writes, "It would appear that the Naval Reserves, despite their war-like proclivities, were regarded hereabouts as the 'pantywaists'...and subjected to much ridicule...Some people even called them the Champagne Preserves, in token of their aristocratic forbears." But later, when the crew covered themselves with glory, that was to change, and the *Yosemite*'s sailors received a tremendous reception from the city.

From Detroit, the crew shipped to Norfolk, Virginia, and first stepped aboard the *Yosemite* on May 7, 1898. They were put under the command of a regular navy officer, William Emory, and after some sea trials were assigned to the Eastern Squadron, heading to Key West by the end of May.

The *Yosemite* had been acquired by the navy from the Southern Pacific Company and renamed on April 13, 1898. The 6,100-ton ship was 389 feet long and could make a top speed of sixteen knots. It was outfitted with ten five-inch guns, six six-pound guns and a pair of Colt Gatling–type guns. It had no armor plating but used coal bags to protect the engines and the main deck.

Early in June, the *Yosemite* and its crew arrived off Havana before heading to Santiago and then Guantanamo Bay. It was there that the ship took part in its first action, acting as an escort to a transport ship carrying a marine battalion of 650 men.

On June 10, prior to the landing, the *Yosemite* shelled the beach for over half an hour. One of the ship's landing boats brought the first group of marines ashore, and according to one source, a U of M man then planted the first American flag on Cuban soil. Crew members also helped capture a small Spanish cannon.

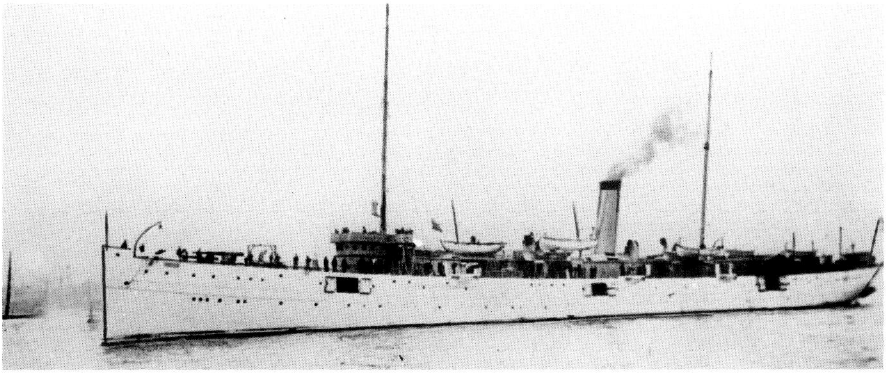

The USS *Yosemite* off the waters of Cuba. *Burton Historical Collection, Detroit Public Library.*

The next day, the *Yosemite* was ordered to clear a path through a minefield in the bay's main channel. The task was handled by a small team that included Charles B. King, a future DAC member and the man credited with first driving a gasoline-powered automobile on the streets of Detroit four years earlier. Using the *Yosemite*'s steam launch and hidden by the cover of darkness, the mission went well until the boat ran aground near a Spanish fort. A tense few moments passed before the launch slipped away unnoticed.

Other U.S. ships arrived to support the landing force, and the *Yosemite* was given a new assignment. On June 16–17, the ship was involved in a minor controversy—a failed attempt to intercept a Spanish ship known as the *Purissima Concepcion* headed for Kingston, Jamaica. According to DAC member Joseph Stringham's self-published memoir, *The Story of the* Yosemite, published in 1929, the crew "missed capturing this Spanish prize through some unexplained carelessness or bungling by the officers on watch."

Stringham was known as a "jack-o-the-dust" on the *Yosemite* and was in charge of the food, small stores and supplies. After the war, he became a member of the Detroit Board of Education and a research engineer with the city. He also served as an ordnance officer with the army during World War I.

Early in the morning of June 16, the officers on watch, including Henry Joy, sighted a large vessel that was quickly identified as the *Concepcion*. Joy and his fellow officers sent word to Emory's cabin, but the captain never ordered a pursuit, and the Spanish ship vanished. Arriving in Kingston, the crew was informed that they had just missed the Spanish ship.

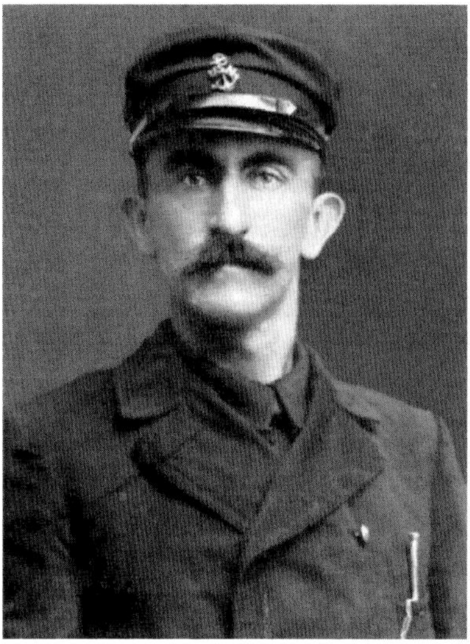

Yosemite chief boatswain's mate Henry B. Joy, future two-time DAC president. *Burton Historical Collection, Detroit Public Library.*

Emory's explanation that "heavy weather" prevented clear identification was written in the official record, but Joy was so incensed about the issue that he wrote his own tale of the incident, which was published by his wife, Helen Newberry Joy, after his death in 1936. In the book, Joy disputes Stringham's insinuation that the "officers of the watch" were at fault. Joy claims that Emory remained in his quarters when informed about the approaching ship, doing nothing more than looking out a porthole several times to peer in the direction of the vessel. Joy writes, "Three times [we] called to the orderly to alert the captain of the escaping ship, but there was no reply from Emory."

A few days after the incident, the *Yosemite* was sent to Puerto Rico to help blockade San Juan Harbor. Blockade life was dull, but Stringham reports that the crew would receive visits from native "bum boats" selling tobacco, cigarettes, fruit and trinkets. He writes, "On two occasions each member of the crew was allowed one bottle of beer for five cents...and much bargaining and trading were carried on by some in order to obtain more than one bottle."

Two sharks were caught at sea by trolling with iron hooks forged on board and baited with salt pork. Efforts to cook the shark proved the meat "unpalatable."

By the afternoon of June 26, the *Yosemite*'s fame was about to be etched in naval records. A second blockade ship, the *St. Paul*, had departed that morning, leaving the *Yosemite* alone to watch the harbor, which was protected by Morro Castle fort and sheltered two enemy cruisers and two other gunboats.

The ship spent several days chasing merchant ships, but then, on the morning of June 28, the *Yosemite* went to chase a blockade runner, the *Antonio Lopez*, doing so right through the harbor fort's zone of fire. When it didn't stop, the *Yosemite* opened fire, sending the *Lopez* reeling toward cover of the fort, where it ran aground. As the *Yosemite* approached and continued to fire, puffs of white smoke were sighted from the Spanish fort, and shells began to land near the *Yosemite*.

As Emory put the ship in a zigzag, three Spanish warships emerged from the harbor and opened fire, forcing the *Yosemite* to deeper water. One member of the *Yosemite* later wrote, "Think of [us], a merchant ship, manned by a green, non-professional crew, with three men-o-war, a troopship and a very powerful fort for enemies, [and] standing off the whole lot."

In spite of heavy fire from the fort and the Spanish ships, the *Yosemite* still pounded the *Lopez* to pieces and began to return fire on the warships emerging from the harbor. Denby described the action, saying that the *Yosemite*'s fire "was too rapid and accurate" for the Spanish ships, one of which began to list heavily.

Shortly after, the Spanish ships retreated, leaving the *Lopez* battered and useless. The *Yosemite* had heavily damaged two of the three enemy vessels while surviving the fight virtually unscathed (no shell hit the ship). The crew continued flying its battle flags the rest of the day, waiting for the Spanish to come back out of the harbor and continue the struggle, but they remained behind the guns of Morro Castle.

For their heroic "one-ship war" against the Spanish navy, the crewmen were given a cash reward of three months' pay, the only extra prize money given out during the entire war and the last such money ever given by the U.S. military. Each sailor also received two medals for his efforts during the entire campaign.

Not long after the fight, on July 4, the crew held "field games" on the deck with "bottles of beer, cooled in the sea" as the principal prizes. Then, on July 15, the *Yosemite* was relieved of blockade duty and ordered to join a fleet at Newport News, Virginia, preparing to sail for Spain. After the surrender of Santiago by the Spanish, the *Yosemite* crew was discharged from duty and returned home to Detroit. Before their return to Detroit, Emory mustered the crewmen and told them how proud he was of "their coolness and enthusiasm under fire" and their "cheerful" performance under trying tropical conditions.

The homecoming on August 21 was a great event in Detroit. Cheering throngs lined Fort Street from the Michigan Central Railroad Depot to Woodward Avenue while the sailors marched to city hall and the Soldiers Monument. They were later dismissed at the very same dock where their adventure had begun a few months earlier. Stark wrote in his book about Detroit that the "pantywaists were the heroes of the town when they came marching home."

The *Yosemite* remained in U.S. Navy service until 1900, when it was badly damaged in a typhoon off the island of Guam and scuttled. Its exact location remains unknown. Today, another navy ship wears the proud name of Yosemite.

Little noticed, a spent shell casing from one of the *Yosemite*'s five-inch guns can still be seen in the lobby of the Detroit Club, carved with the names of members of the crew. A plaque, dedicated by Charles King on the golden anniversary of the *Yosemite*, can be found at the Naval Reserve Armory near the Belle Isle Bridge, but few other artifacts from the splendid ship exist.

Chapter 8

THE FOUNDING OF A MODERN DAC

Even with all its athletic teams and leading sports figures tearing it up across the nation, the DAC was already in trouble by the mid-1890s. Lobbying to create a downtown DAC (either on the riverfront or along Woodward but closer to Grand Circus Park) nearly tore apart the ranks of the membership.

In his brief history of the DAC for the first "Roster" issue of the *DAC News* in 1919, past president Hugh Chalmers said that both Henry Joy and first club president Frederick Stearns were advocating a downtown club. Joy was asked to run for the presidency in 1894, at a time when having two candidates was unheard of (the rightful president-to-be was Dwight Rexford). His platform included pushing for a new DAC downtown, and even though he won the vote, the idea was bitterly debated before being thrown on the dust pile of history. Lodge said that Joy tried to revisit the issue again in 1896, suggesting a clubhouse and athletic field on the riverfront. But, he noted, "the reactionaries won the campaign and the dream was never realized."

Later, Joy would write Chalmers about joining a new DAC. "Have been a member of the DAC for 30 years," he wrote. "Tried my level best to get a permanent clubhouse for it then, but was 30 years ahead of the times… There is a magic spell in the letters DAC, and if it can be arranged to keep the name and the historic organization…it will be a loadstone to attract the support of hundreds who would swing into line again as DAC members who might not take any interest in a new name and organization."

At the end of the letter, Joy, a football star of the first DAC, asked to be listed as the first member of the new club. And he was.

When the Spanish-American War began in 1898, members of Detroit's elite signed up to fight. Many had been involved in the Michigan Naval Reserve, and by 1899, the war had drained away more than 100 of the DAC's brightest and best, a loss from which the old DAC never fully recovered. There were about 350 members at the time. While the DAC continued to field strong athletic teams for many years, the property deteriorated and the clubhouse was neglected.

John Kelsey's generosity kept the club in operation and fielding quality baseball, basketball and football teams. On the inside, the club was in deep trouble, but to the community, the DAC remained a dominant athletic force, daily being featured on the growing sports pages of the city's newspapers.

As the twentieth century dawned, Kelsey repeatedly fought proposals to close the club's doors. He personally covered the club's operating debt year after year (often as much as $15,000), hoping that someday the DAC would get new life in downtown Detroit. He was quoted as saying, "We've got to keep the old club alive because someday we'll rebuild and have the finest athletic club in America."

Besides the rapidly changing nature of sports (more collegiate activities, fewer clubs), the Woodward Avenue clubhouse just had way too little in the way of revenue-producing facilities. Eddie Batchelor noted that the original DAC had "no bar; no sleeping accommodations, no restaurant…it had to depend largely for money to pay operating expenses on the sale of tickets to athletic events. The trouble was that seating for spectators was so limited that the returns were meager."

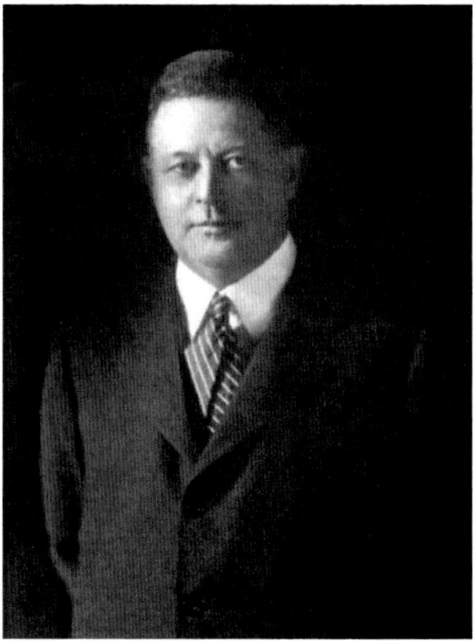

DAC baseball star John Kelsey kept the club going in the 1900s. *DAC archives.*

In the same article, Batchelor adamantly writes that the present DAC was in no "sense the natural heir of the first one. All that it inherited was the name." But in a *DAC News* article from 1965, the opposite view is expressed: "The origin of the present Club must be sought in the characters of those men who had been members of that older DAC uptown. They were anything but common men."

It was during the time of the DAC's great basketball teams in the early twentieth century that events were taking place that would culminate in the birth of a new DAC.

By early 1912, the DAC had virtually ceased to exist, even though John Kelsey was still president (he had sustained the battered club for a decade), William Ducharme (a DAC baseball star) was vice-president and John Lodge was the club captain. The catalyst in setting in motion a new club was Charles A. Hughes. Hughes was one of the new auto insiders, a former advertising manager at Hudson Motor Car, hired by college friend Roy Chapin. So it was on the day before Thanksgiving, November 27, 1912, that the first meeting of sixteen men was held in the Pontchartrain Hotel to discuss a new club, with Charles A. Hughes acting as secretary. The ad hoc group contained some original DAC members and auto industry and business leaders. Athletic prowess was not a significant factor in the group's makeup. After informal discussion, it was decided to form a committee of seven to put a club scheme into operation. At that moment, the new DAC was conceived, with goals and members, in a city vastly different from what it was when the first DAC was born twenty-five years earlier.

There must have been considerable informal discussions among the new DAC proponents before that first meeting, for in attendance was Harry J. Porter, president of the Wolverine Automobile Club, suggesting that the new club take over its property located at the northeast corner of John R. and Madison Avenue. Hughes made a motion for taking over the Wolverine property for $108,500 plus commissions and other incidental expenses, and it was passed. It was a remarkably bold move for a nonexistent club with no funding to take without the clear understanding of the members present that a new downtown Detroit Athletic Club was a foregone conclusion. The *Detroit News*, *Times* and *Free Press* were quick to pick up on the story and ran extensive articles the following day saying essentially that a new DAC Clubhouse costing $750,000 was to be built on Madison Avenue.

In December 1912, Kelsey sent out a notice to the remaining members calling for a meeting to dissolve the corporation and dispose of any remaining assets. Kelsey was credited by some with getting a "head of steam" behind the move to transfer the name and goodwill of the original club.

Also that month, the organization committee moved to elect Hughes as club secretary, and work began to prepare for a charter-signing meeting on January 4, 1913, at the Pontchartrain Hotel. At that meeting, 109 men were invited to be charter members (including many from the original Woodward DAC), but only 107 signed new articles of incorporation.

At the same time, $500 a month was assessed to each of the ten organization committee members, and it was agreed that the Wolverine Club be purchased as the future site of the club. Additionally, a holding company was created to buy the site, and incorporation papers were ready to be signed when 107 charter incorporators were selected.

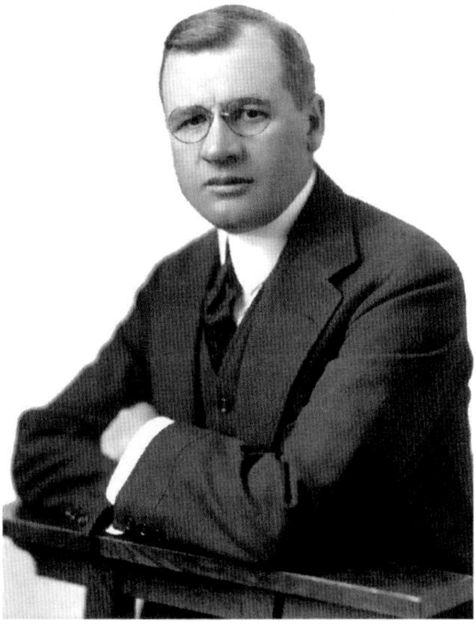

Hugh Chalmers, first president of the modern DAC (1913–16). *DAC archives.*

The charter-signing meeting also produced a powerhouse board of directors consisting of eighteen men: Hugh Chalmers, Roy D. Chapin, Emory W. Clark, George P. Codd, Frank W. Eddy, David Gray, N.A. Hawkins, Frederick H. Holt, Henry B. Joy, John Kelsey, Abner E. Larned, E.W. Lewis, William E. Metzger, William R. Orr, G.D. Pope, W.E. Scripps, Neil W. Snow and R.B. Tannahill. Hugh Chalmers, president of Chalmers Motor Co., was elected president (serving two consecutive terms); Henry B. Joy, chairman of the board of Packard Motor Co., was vice-president; Emory Clark, president of First National Bank, was second vice-president; Norval Hawkins, Ford sales manager, was treasurer; and Charles A. Hughes was secretary.

On January 10, 1913, the original Woodward Avenue DAC was formally dissolved and all the club trophies turned over to the new DAC. The timing clearly shows that there was no break in the use of the Detroit Athletic Club name; indeed, there was a six-day period when both the old and new clubs apparently coexisted.

Just over a month later, on February 22, 1913, the DAC basketball team, which was still playing, was sent notice by Hughes, as organizing secretary, to stop using the DAC name pending the team members' admittance into the re-formed Detroit Athletic Club.

It's not clear how the original DAC property was disposed of, but eventually it was sold. For a time, various sports and commercial interests were operated there, including Convention Hall, a large auditorium popular as a meeting place and showroom. Today, the site just north of the Whitney restaurant is owned by Wayne State.

Inevitably, it was a sad ending for a club that had truly brought championship sports to Detroit while forging the way for Detroit to become known on the national athletic stage. In the end, perhaps Kelsey said it best about that first DAC: "The honors this club has brought to Detroit mean too much to let them die now."

The clearest possible indication, however, of how the new club differed from the old came in a statement that appeared in the February 14, 1913 *Detroit Times*: "The DAC will make no attempt to startle the world with world record runners, champion basketball, football, or baseball teams."

With so many high-visibility people involved, word regarding the formation of a new DAC and the people behind it quickly spread, aided by extensive press coverage. In February, the *Detroit News* reported 300 new DAC members and indicated that an equal number would be enrolled at the next board meeting, making it, in one month's time, the largest club in Detroit. The pace of applications prompted the board to announce the raising of the entrance fee to $200 once 1,000 members were enrolled, prompting a new onslaught of entries. By February 24, the club had 885 members and expected to reach 1,000 by March 1.

Meanwhile, applications from Detroit's best citizens continued to arrive at the DAC office at 318 Majestic Building. Membership chairman Roy Chapin remarked, "Among the applicants are several hundred of the best-known men in the city." The 1,000-member level was reached by March 6, and when the previously determined maximum of 1,500 resident members was certain by March 9, 1913, the Membership Committee, its work done, resigned.

The year 1914 was a momentous time in the world and for the DAC. On January 22, just five days before the annual meeting, Director Neil W. Snow died. At the annual meeting on January 27, it was decided, with 1,487 already on the rolls, to amend the bylaws to increase the resident membership limit from 1,500 to 2,000. The club's action was reported in all Detroit papers, which also indicated that there were 200 prospective members on a waiting list.

On June 12, Frank W. Eddy, the key founder of the 1887 DAC and a board member of the new club, died of a sudden heart attack at age sixty-three.

By the fall, construction was set to begin on the new clubhouse.

Chapter 9

HOOPS PIONEER LED DAC SQUAD

As the April winds blew cold, a record crowd packed Detroit's Moose Temple to watch the end of one of the city's best-known sports franchises, the DAC Deltas basketball team, in the 1913 state championship. By night's end, the Deltas were disbanded as the last vestige of the old Detroit Athletic Club. Named after the Greek letter—the triangle still incorporated in the club's logo—the Deltas were defending their AAU title.

Proudly playing guard was the five-foot, ten-inch Jacob "Jake" Mazer, the founder of the DAC team, acknowledged as one of Michigan's greatest early athletes and later called the "great-grandfather of Detroit basketball." His teammates did not tower up to seven feet, either, but played like they were giants.

Managing the Deltas was Fred M. Shinnick, who would later captain the club's championship bowling team. The Deltas were favorites, having won the 1912 regional championship.

Facing the Deltas were the "hardware boys" from T.B. Rayl's, a team they had defeated twice during their nearly cancelled season. Coincidentally, the Rayl's team was owned by DAC member Dudley Wetmore Smith.

In a brief existence from 1901 through 1913, the Deltas set an impressive record for amateur basketball and are part of a nearly forgotten chapter of basketball history. At one point, they won one hundred consecutive games over three years and even defeated Yale twice. The "DAC five" trounced competitors from the YMCA, Michigan State Agricultural College, Notre Dame, Michigan State Normal College (forerunner of Eastern Michigan), Hillsdale, Albion and Adrian.

Detroit was one of the early hotspots for basketball, a game invented at Springfield College in Massachusetts in 1892. In Detroit, the first hoop games were played at the YMCA.

Mazer is credited with organizing the DAC team in 1902. Later, he owned Detroit's first professional basketball team, the Eagles, which played at the old Light Guard Armory. Born in the Ukraine in 1877, Mazer immigrated to America four years later with his family, settling in Pittsburgh, where his father opened a cigar factory. He learned the trade from his father and made a name for himself as a bicycle racer in Pittsburgh, where he also learned basketball. By the time he arrived in Detroit in 1900 to open a cigar factory with his brother, Henry, Mazer was a seasoned player who could shoot baskets from any part of the gym with his eyes closed.

After his first season, Mazer left the YMCA in a dispute and started the rival DAC team, taking several players with him. They included the six-foot-tall Dr. C. Bradford Lundy, center; a balding Shinnick, who played forward; Clarence Lidington, the second defensive guard, who went on to work at Detroit Edison for forty-two years; and John Richards as right forward.

Soon, the DAC was recognized as having some of Detroit's best-known basketball players, defeating foes far and wide. Lundy was a 1904 graduate of the Detroit College of Medicine. A native of Detroit, he was tapped by

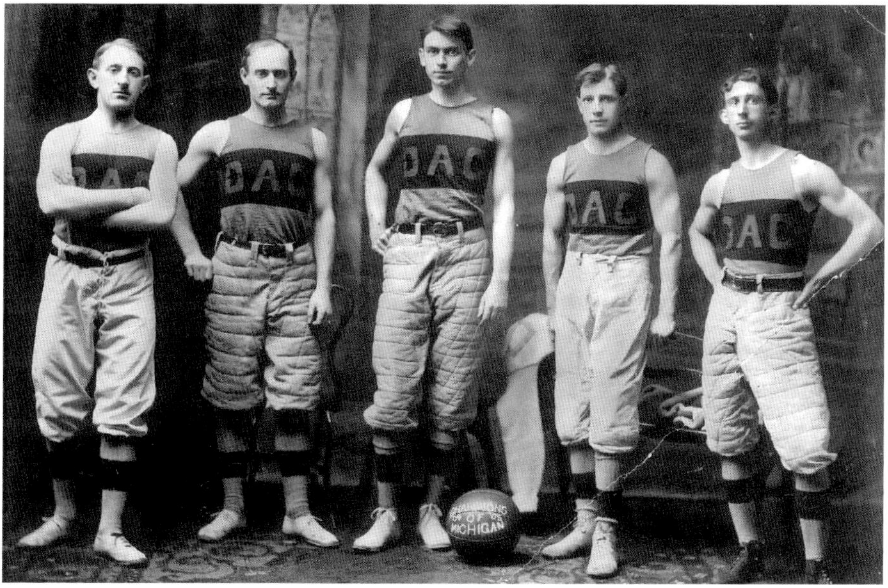

Basketball pioneer Jake Mazer (far left) and DAC teammates. *DAC archives.*

Mayor James Couzens to run the city's recreation department during World War I. Shinnick was an executive at Briggs Manufacturing and later Detroit's Central Iron Foundry, from which he retired in 1945.

The five were "iron men" on the court, playing four consecutive seasons together without a single substitution. This was also the time the Deltas racked up their string of one hundred victories, ended by a defeat to their archrival foes at the local YMCA.

In 1904–5, the Deltas defeated all local contenders and won the state title before facing Yale. It was generally believed that the Detroiters were overreaching in challenging the doughty Elis and that the crowd that packed the Light Guard Armory would see the home talent butchered. Instead, the Deltas pulled an upset. Mazer hounded Kinney, Yale's big scorer, while Yale's Foster Rockwell subdued Shinnick. The squeaker was decided when Shinnick was fouled just as the final whistle blew and Mazer cashed in for the point and a 24–23 victory. Overall, Mazer sank sixteen free throws.

The Deltas also split two games with Notre Dame's team during one of its seasons, helping place Detroit basketball on the national map.

The "war on the floor" during the Deltas' time was closer to today's sport than when basketball was first invented. Originally, the game's inventor set up peach baskets mounted on poles. By 1897, the backboard had been added, but it wasn't until 1914—after the Deltas were disbanded—that a hole was cut in the bottom of the basket so the ball could fall through instead of requiring a player to poke it out. Public interest was only behind football and baseball for the fast game, played in two twenty-minute halves separated by a ten-minute break.

Yale and the Deltas played a rematch later in 1905. While Yale had a number of new players, Mazer and his teammates stayed together and beat the Ivy Leaguers 19–15. The DAC won the state championship again at season's end.

By 1906, the Deltas and the Detroit YMCA were locked in a cross-city rivalry. The DAC won the 1906 and 1911 city championships, while the YMCA took the 1907 and 1909 series.

A master of the dribble, Mazer was able to put the Deltas ahead due to his uncanny ability to sink free throws. In one city championship game against the YMCA, Mazer sunk a then unheard-of seventeen out of seventeen shots. The DAC men flattened the Detroit Medical College team 72–2.

As business concerns forced some of Mazer's teammates to leave, he remained on the Deltas until the end. Replacement players included the five-foot, eight-inch Roy Boozey, one of Michigan's pioneer greats; George

M. Lawton, one of the finest punters and fullbacks developed by U of M's Fielding H. Yost; Alex MacDiarmid, co-founder of Detroit's MacDiarmid Candy Company; and James Joy Miller, an executive of the Detroit Moving and Storage Company and team captain in 1911–12.

A member of the famed 1909 Wolverines that only suffered one loss during the season, Lawton is better known for his football exploits and connections. He went on to coach football at the University of Detroit for a season before a twenty-year coaching career at Assumption College in Windsor.

Although the Deltas won glory for the club, the old organization was dying as many of its members became involved in the hurried pace of the automobile industry. By the 1912–13 season, the basketball team survived only because Mazer and Shinnick paid the costs out of pocket.

The Deltas also faced the prospect of being a team without a home or the ability to use the DAC name. Due to declining fan attendance, the team could no longer afford rent at their former home, a place called the "Palace rink." Due to legal issues, the organizers of the club informed the Deltas in January 1913 that they had to stop using the DAC name although the season wasn't half over. Optimistic, Shinnick continued booking games for the team, calling itself the DAC Old Guard.

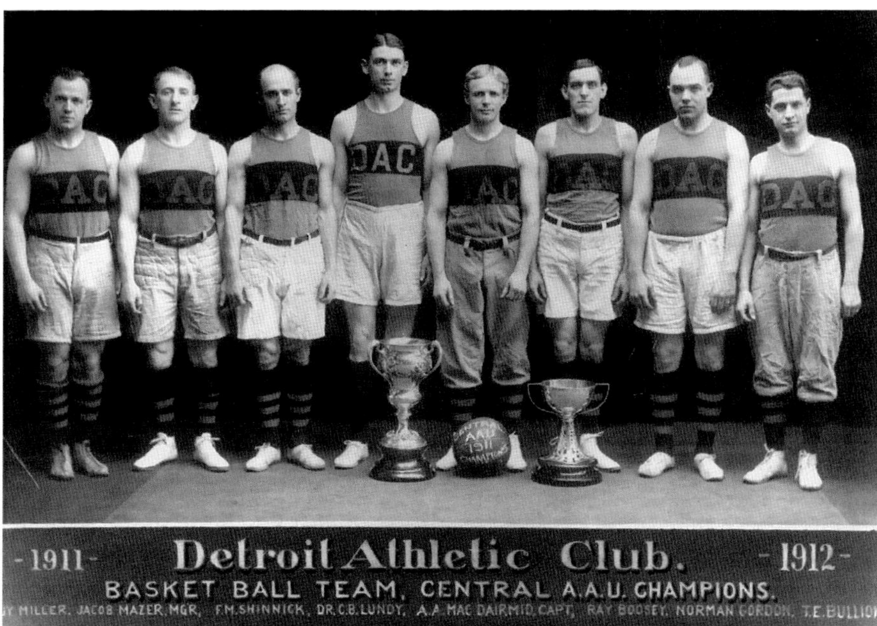

The DAC basketball champions, 1911–12. *DAC archives.*

Playing in the Commercial League, the Deltas had defeated Rayl's Hardware during their first contest in December 1912 and trounced a squad from Alma College 62–14 in January. In what was supposed to be their last game on January 6, 1913, the Deltas again faced the Rayl's team at Holy Rosary school's gym and beat it 31–29.

Instead of disbanding, a deal was worked out allowing the team to continue using the DAC name for the rest of the season. As the season drew to a close, the Deltas made it to the state championship against Rayl's. At the end of the first half, the Deltas were down by one point, 11–10. Six minutes into the second half, Rayl's forward Tom Powers was ejected after he took a swing at Miller. The players were comparatively matched for most of the game, and Mazer scored 13 points. In the end, however, the "hardware boys" rallied in the last minutes of play, beating the Deltas in the 21–20 upset.

After the Deltas disbanded, Mazer and Boozey joined the YMCA team. Mazer continued playing until 1918, when he retired after his team won the state championship.

It is not clear if Mazer, one of Michigan's first great Jewish athletes, was invited to join the re-formed DAC, but he did became president and treasurer of the Detroit AAU, president of the Downtown YMCA Businessmen's Club, chairman of the AAU basketball committee and a member of the American Olympic Committee, and he helped organize the Cadillac Athletic Club, which went bankrupt during the Depression despite Mazer's paying its $400,000 in debts.

Age did not seem to slow his abilities. During his fiftieth birthday celebration on January 5, 1927, he shot fifty consecutive free throws. Three years later, Mazer led his old DAC teammates to victory over Ypsilanti Normal College alumni. Organizing what is supposed to have been Detroit's first professional basketball team, the Eagles, Mazer was both coach and owner. The Eagles started playing in 1939 at the Detroit Light Guard Armory. The team only lasted a couple of years. Mazer died on July 26, 1958, at eighty-one and was posthumously inducted into the Michigan Sports Hall of Fame in 1967.

The old Deltas were gone after the original club faded, but Shinnick and Lundy joined the new DAC and put together another team. A story in a 1916 edition of the *DAC News* noted that the Deltas basketball team cinched another victory on April 27 against Michigan State Normal, 28–26, in a stubbornly fought battle.

It is not known how long the second team played. There apparently weren't enough fans in Detroit to sustain a professional team until the Pistons moved from Fort Wayne in 1957.

Chapter 10

A MAGNIFICENT HOME ON MADISON

As the final exterior touches of the $1.3 million DAC Clubhouse took shape in the autumn of 1914, excitement was reaching a fevered pitch among those eager for a glimpse of Detroit's newest gem. It would be spring before the luxurious edifice designed by Albert Kahn officially debuted, but skilled tradesmen, artisans and craftsmen were hard at work creating a building that is as impressive today as it was when a horse and carriage was a common sight on Madison Avenue. One of the finest buildings in the city, it combines simplicity, utility and beauty of design and furnishings, as alluring now as when the first members passed through the doors in April 1915.

Charles Hughes, a founding member who served as club secretary and publisher of the *DAC News*, knew the club would wield a powerful influence fueled by members from the top echelons of society. The re-formed club was launched when Detroit was the global center of all things automotive. Largely on Hughes's initiative, on the Wednesday before Thanksgiving 1912, sixteen businessmen assembled at the Pontchartrain Hotel and laid plans for the club. The idea had been percolating for years among men like Henry Joy, John Kelsey, Abner Larned, Harry Jewett and Frederick Stearns. Finally, all the essential elements—public support, financing and civic pride—gelled.

Gustavus Pope, soon to be president of the Detroit Society of Arts and Crafts, chaired the first meeting of the DAC organization. He named Hugh Chalmers, president of Chalmers Motor Company, to head a committee to start the ball rolling. The committee sent a letter to members of several Detroit social clubs inviting all to a buffet luncheon on December 7, 1912, at the Pontchartrain and an opportunity to join as incorporators.

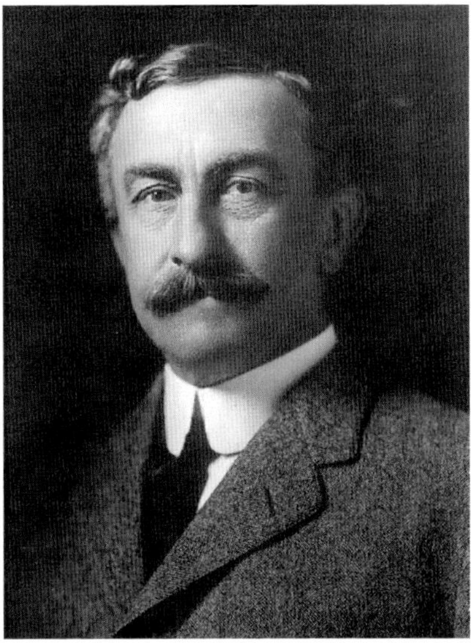

Henry B. Joy, modern DAC member number one. *DAC archives.*

This new DAC was created because so many men had fond memories of the first club and its halcyon days. Packard Motor Company president Henry Joy was one of the original club's stars of the gridiron and a longtime advocate for a downtown DAC. At the December 7 meeting, Joy pledged $10,000, and his enthusiasm rallied subscribers to add another $53,000 before the gavel hit the table. His exuberance also led to Joy's being listed as DAC member number one—sending the committee a $200 check even before an application form had been printed.

Another early supporter was John Kelsey, founder of Kelsey Wheel Company and a gifted ballplayer who helped the original club win two national baseball titles. This self-made millionaire who single-handedly sustained the original club through more than a decade of decline served on both the organizing and building committees and as DAC president in 1917 and 1918.

Jewett was one of the famous "four horsemen" who excelled in track and field. He was on the first DAC athletic committee and served as club president in 1924.

The organization committee set an initiation fee of $100, with annual dues of $60 and a resident member cap of 1,500. As the membership level reached 1,000, the initiation fee was doubled. When the club opened, there were 2,000 resident members and 500 nonresidents.

Still-familiar names like Alger, Bagley, Book, Buhl, Fisher, Larned, Mack, Navin, Skillman, Scripps and Whitney joined early. Even before 1913 dawned, a nominating committee prepared a slate of candidates for the first board of directors, and committees swung into action.

On Saturday, January 4, 1913, 107 civic leaders met to sign the articles of association. Six days later, the original DAC was dissolved and its colors and insignia adopted by the new club, underscoring an ongoing link between the two.

With the organizing committee laying groundwork, just four days after incorporation, the clubhouse site committee was authorized to make an offer on land on the northeast corner of Randolph and Madison. Once optioned by the Wolverine Automobile Club, a failing entity that later reorganized as the Automobile Club of Michigan, this parcel was the first piece among several that would give the DAC the entire block.

Hugh Chalmers was named president; Joy, first vice-president; bank president Emory Clark, second vice-president; Ford Motor executive Norval Hawkins, treasurer; and Hughes, secretary.

The president of the struggling Wolverine Automobile Club (WAC) negotiated the transaction that saw the DAC take over the site for $116,000. The WAC attracted many of the same auto executives who joined the DAC.

In total, the DAC paid $308,000 to secure all the land necessary, paying one-third for a single lot on Randolph owned by the hard-bargaining Alex Fowler. Knowing how badly the DAC wanted his land, Fowler stood firm in his demand for $100,000, about twice its worth, and after much wrangling, the DAC finally capitulated.

When the wrecking ball arrived in late September 1913, rooming houses and a blacksmith shop were among the fifteen buildings razed.

The field of architects to build this grand monument was narrowed to two candidates: the firms of Albert Kahn or Smith, Hinchman and Grylls. After hearing presentations by both in March 1913, the board voted unanimously for Kahn. A pioneer in the use of reinforced concrete and open interior spaces, Kahn incorporated these details into the DAC's plans. That spring, Kahn accompanied the building committee to athletic clubs in several cities for inspiration. The DAC Clubhouse would be elegant and refined, comfortable and magnificent, efficient and effective.

It took Kahn several months to complete plans for the building (six floors plus two mezzanine levels). On June 20, 1913, he presented plans inspired by Italian Renaissance palaces, with construction costs projected at $750,000 for the 160,000-square-foot facility. It was determined that the building façade be of Bedford limestone, creating a rich and dignified appearance with sufficient lawn and splendid elm trees.

The main entrance would be on Madison Avenue and would open to a large hall. Kahn's main lobby was a spacious room in the Italian Renaissance style with walls wainscoted to the ceiling with large panels of American walnut, floors of patterned gray Tennessee marble and an imposing fireplace of Hauteville marble. Farther in, elevators and a grand staircase anchored both sides of the lobby, connecting the entrance hall with the Grill Room designed after a famous fourteenth-century palace near Florence.

The ladies' entrance was planned on the Randolph side of the building, which would also serve as the carriage and automobile entrance. In addition to the superbly crafted Main Dining Room, there was the Palm Room, the ladies' dining room and three private dining rooms.

The third level offered a modern Turkish bath department with lockers, a dressing room, game and card rooms and additional private dining rooms. The much-anticipated swimming pool or "plunge" occupied practically the entire south front of the fourth floor, accentuated by massive arched windows. It was one of the first pools in the country to be built above the first floor of a building. There was also a gymnasium, along with a handball and two squash courts.

Two upper levels would house 108 sleeping rooms and suites of varying sizes, most with private bathrooms. On the first mezzanine there was to be a library, manager's office and boardroom. A rooftop garden with pergola, basement bowling alley and trophy room finished the plans.

In November 1913, charter member Robert Tannahill negotiated the purchase of a lot with eighty feet of frontage on Randolph to be used as a club garage.

It was estimated that the building would be completed by Christmas 1914. In the interim, the DAC kept a business office in the Majestic building, where applications for membership flowed.

First mortgage bonds totaling $500,000 were to be held by financial institutions, including First National Bank. The finance committee abandoned a members-only investment policy, and local banks and trusts bought large individual shares. A second bond issue for $600,000 was to be raised through the membership and was completed in what became the most talked about sales meeting of the era. On December 16, 1913, at the board of commerce convention hall, banker Emory Clark explained the financing scheme to one thousand eager attendees. Next, Henry Joy and John Lodge, early DAC athletes, reminisced about the first club's glory days. But the piece de resistance that evening was the performance of founding member Abner Larned.

Following a lantern slideshow by architect Kahn, who unveiled the elaborate plans to palpable excitement, Larned demonstrated his amazing salesmanship while directors locked the doors, literally holding the audience captive. Undoubtedly using the same techniques that enabled him to raise

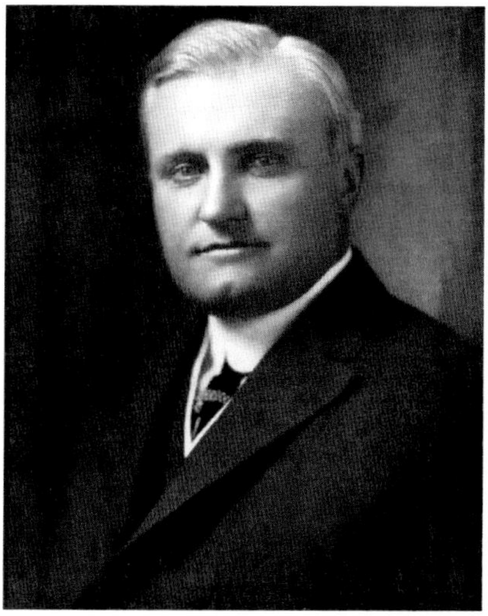

Abner Larned, the DAC's extraordinary salesman. *DAC archives.*

funds to launch the Detroit YMCA in 1909 and manage a $2 million drive for Wayne County roads, Larned raised all the cash needed for the DAC in two hours. In a frenzied style similar to a church revival, with directors scattered throughout the cavernous hall, members pledged from $500 to $15,000 to secure the remaining $290,000 in bonds; the balance had been raised by enthusiastic supporters in the first month after organization. With that goal met, Chalmers and Joy led a snake dance through downtown streets in happy celebration. The amount raised assured that the project could move forward. The next day, Hughes was instructed to solicit subscriptions by mail from nonresident members.

When the dust settled, there was $50,000 shrinkage in subscriptions. By dint of doorbell ringing, $15,000 was raised, but the club still faced a deficit. Harry Jewett called his friend Harvey Firestone, a nonresident member and founder of Firestone Tire and Rubber, who agreed to buy the balance.

On the day after Larned's successful fundraising spectacle, the *Detroit Journal* published an editorial chiding the elite club for its luxurious indulgence while a downtown hotel for working women struggled to raise the last $5,000 necessary to launch debt free. DAC members responded by immediately raising the funds necessary for the Priscilla Inn, which opened debt free on New Year's Day 1914.

By January, the clubhouse was taking shape, if only on blueprints. Some twenty-two builders nationwide made bids on construction. The directors wanted a Detroit project from start to finish, even offering to make up the difference if a local firm was not the lowest bidder.

After two days of review, the board awarded the contract to the Vinton Company of Detroit for $640,000. Robert Vinton, grandson of the company founder, was a third-generation builder. The physical structure of the DAC was in experienced hands.

The building would have a steel framework with reinforced concrete, the exterior of brick and stone. Every detail of finish and equipment was

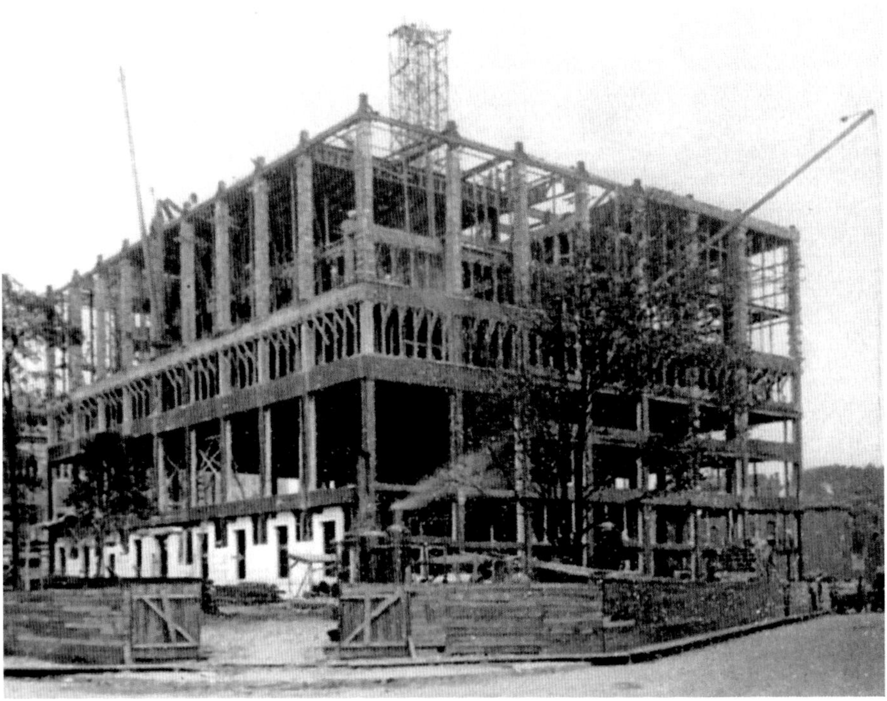

The steel frame of the clubhouse takes shape. *DAC archives.*

to be the most modern obtainable. In January 1914, newspapers were reporting that Vinton planned to have the clubhouse ready for occupancy by Christmas. More than forty sub-contractor and supplier companies joined in. The project required 1,350 tons of structural steel framework. Except for a delay in delivery of steel, there were no major snags, yet the clubhouse wasn't ready until April 1915.

Every modern convenience was planned by Kahn. A low-voltage switchboard in the basement engineering department controlled all three thousand lights in the building. The steam heating system employed fifty-six electric motors. The kitchen featured electric dishwashers, ovens—even a mechanical potato peeler.

As the clubhouse rose, construction equipment dotted the downtown skyline, with the Statler and Tuller hotels, the David Whitney and the Kresge buildings going up. The Detroit Board of Commerce noted that Detroit was fourth in the nation in respect to building activity, surpassed only by New York, Chicago and Philadelphia.

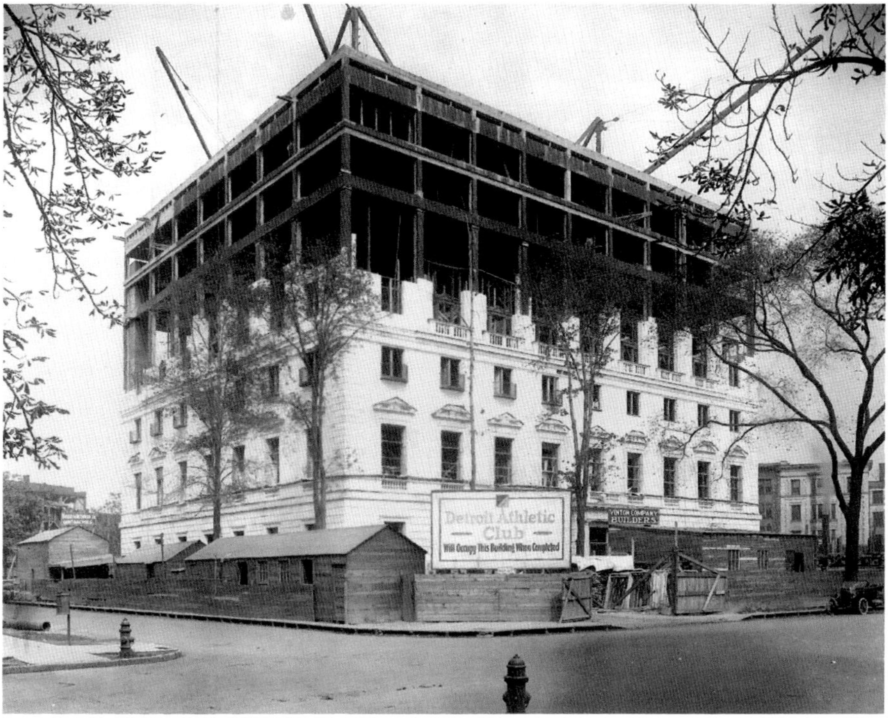

Construction moves along as the exterior takes shape. *DAC archives.*

By mid-April 1914, the foundation and basement were underway. Before the Fourth of July, workers were adding a support layer for the seventy-five-by twenty-five-foot swimming pool. It was formed of a waterproof steel tank resting on structural steel framing and covered with reinforced concrete. On August 13, the exterior limestone façade was started from grade to cornice on all sides with entrance steps of granite. The exterior shell inched its way toward completion through the fall.

While officials hammered out the big construction issues, much thought was placed on furnishing the clubhouse with the finest silver, china, glassware, linens, kitchen equipment and light fixtures. The board authorized spending $9,000 to build a wine collection, $8,000 for cigars and $3,000 for restaurant stock. The W. & J. Sloane Company of New York was contracted for furnishing and decorating the clubhouse. This Fifth Avenue vendor was charged with placing furniture, carpets, rugs and hangings, as well as color coordination, an $186,000 proposition. In total, the price tag for interior furnishings exceeded $200,000.

By July, in response to so many works of art donated, Henry Joy decreed that no more gifts intended for the club be accepted unless considered first by the house committee.

On January 15, 1915, the club library was launched with a gift of three sets of books from the general manager of *Collier's Weekly*: a deluxe edition of Harvard classics, Henry Cabot Lodge's American history in twenty-five volumes and the junior classics.

Founding member Frederick Stearns offered a bust of Hermes, and C. Harold Wills, one of the designers of Ford's Model T, gifted the club with a handsome Caldwell clock now displayed near the second-floor elevators.

The club's organizing committee was besieged with applications for employment from club managers, athletic directors, swim instructors and chefs across America. Of more than two hundred applicants for clubhouse manager, Alexander Nixon of Boston was selected. A veteran of nineteen years with that city's Algonquin Club, he also managed the New York Athletic Club for six years. Nixon and secretary Hughes became the first two occupants of the new clubhouse in February 1915.

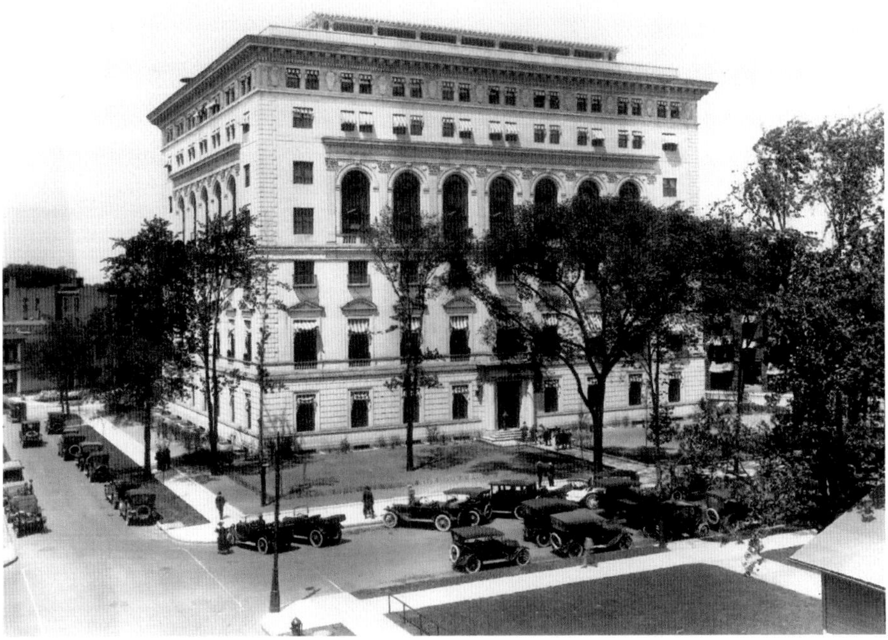

A beautiful new clubhouse in 1915. *DAC archives.*

Edward Caldwell was among a trio of prominent artisans whose creative flourish still commands the attention of visitors. The premier early twentieth-century designer and manufacturer of electric light fixtures and decorative metalworks, Caldwell's mastery is evident in the exquisite chandeliers, lanterns and wall sconces, as well as fireplace andirons and the massive candelabra in the main lobby.

Fresh from illustrating the 1912 edition of Hans Christian Andersen fairytales, British-born painter A. Duncan Carse did extensive frescoes on the Main Dining Room ceiling. With only a few assistants and over just a few months, Carse painted nearly one thousand original pictures, no two alike, including leaves, fruit, parrots, monkeys and athletic contests from early Greek to modern.

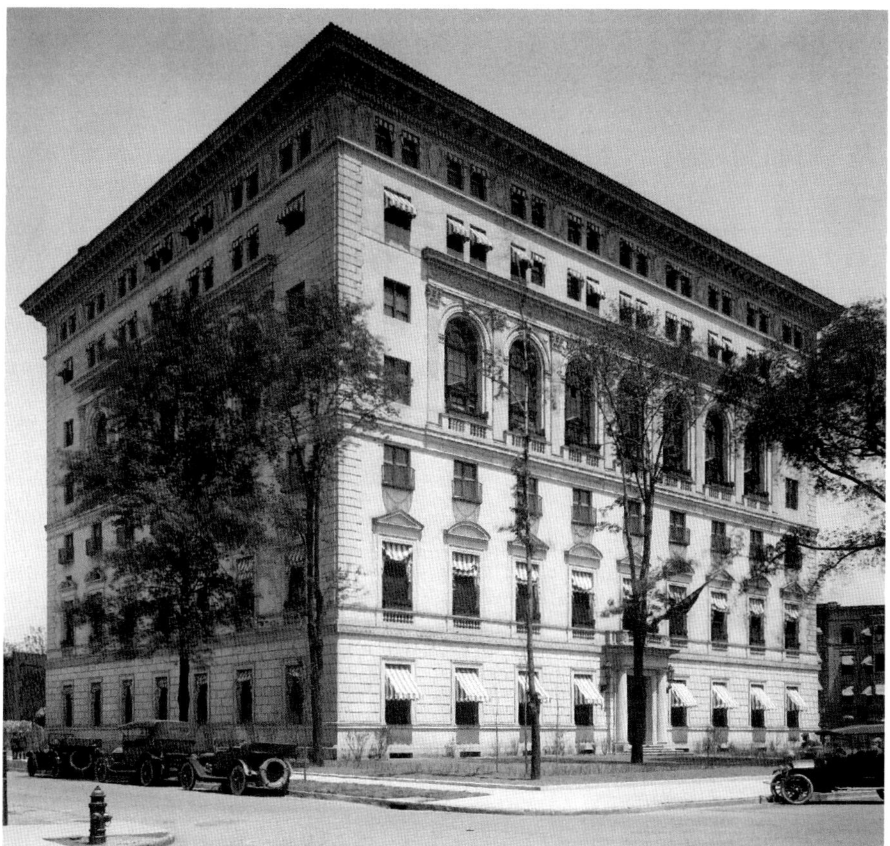

A street-level view of the completed clubhouse. *DAC archives.*

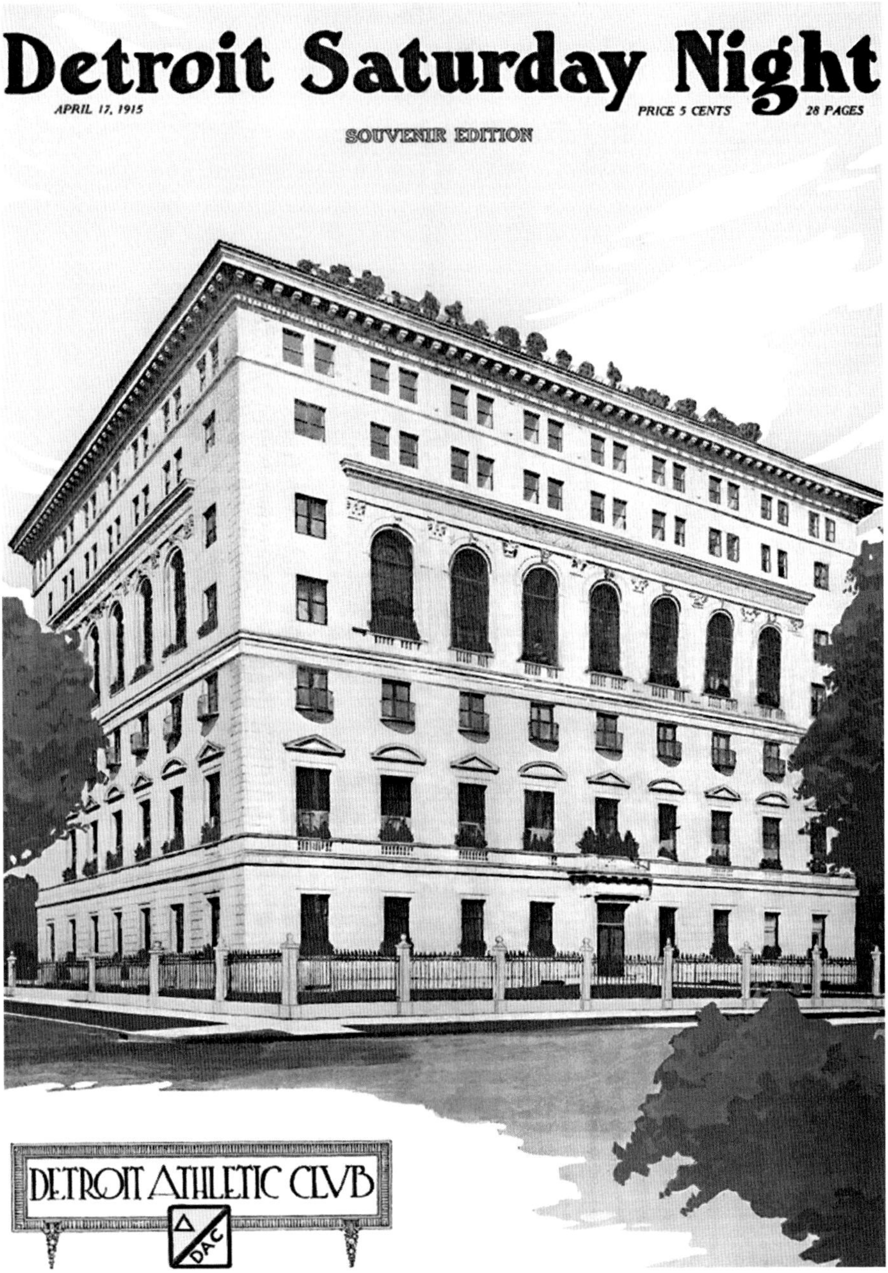

DAC's grand opening stirred media attention, including this *Detroit Saturday Night* cover in April 1915. *DAC archives.*

The beautiful balustrade that frames the grand staircase is the work of Samuel Yellin, called "the Tiffany of metalwork." The wrought-iron railing touched up in dull gold stands out against the marble stairway and is exquisite and stylish, akin to fine jewelry on an architectural scale. Yellin created the wrought-ironwork department at the prestigious Pennsylvania Museum School of Industrial Arts.

Much like the conductor of a symphony orchestra, Kahn oversaw every detail of interior design.

The club staged its first event when eight hundred women attended two demonstrations poolside with Australian swimming star Annette Kellerman on March 26, 1915. The second program was scheduled at the last minute to accommodate the overwhelming turnout. Clad in ankle-length skirts and fancy hats, members' wives and daughters filled seating to capacity for each show.

On April 9, 1915, the DAC closed to members because contractors—carpet installers, drapery hangers and the like—were hampered by too many visitors. The festivities to officially welcome the new DAC commenced on April 15–16. The club was open in readiness, except for the basement bowling alley.

The weekend celebration culminated with a sold-out dinner and concert by the Detroit Symphony Orchestra. No formal ceremony was attempted because the crowd was too large to be comfortably accommodated.

From across the nation, praise poured in. One scribe said the club was "an expression of Detroit's greatness. Nowhere is there a place so elegantly appointed, so convenient, so splendidly equipped." Hugh Chalmers enthused, "The DAC has become recognized all over the world as one of the greatest clubs. It will continue to impress our guests as the crystallized spirit of Detroit."

Chapter 11

HOW DAC MEMBERS CONTROLLED THE AUTO INDUSTRY

When the Detroit Athletic Club opened the doors to its new Madison Avenue clubhouse in April 1915, members of the club controlled over 90 percent of the world's automobile production. By that time, there were 2,010 members in resident and nonresident categories. At the same time, nearly one million cars were rolling out of factories around Detroit and the nation, most of them built by member-owned companies. During the first six years that the club enrolled new members (1913–19) to reach the 2,000 plateau, more than 700 were directly linked to the automobile business—engineering, assembling, selling, distributing and financing cars, as well as the parts and components that made them begin to look like the kind of vehicle we might recognize today.

These seven hundred members were directly involved with over one hundred automobile manufacturing businesses and another one hundred suppliers. All told, the two hundred firms so controlled the automobile business in the United States that before there was a Motor City as the world came to know it, one could have easily called the DAC the "Detroit Automobile Club." And in 1915, many people did just that.

The important thing about the DAC was that it was a place for (auto) people to get together, explained Beverly Kimes, a nationally renowned auto historian and author of a key industry source, the *Standard Catalog of American Cars: 1805–1942*. Before her death, Kimes noted that the DAC members "built a palace to an industry that started as something for backyard tinkering. Its creation showed that the industry was growing up and flexing its muscle. Here they could share ideas and socialize together."

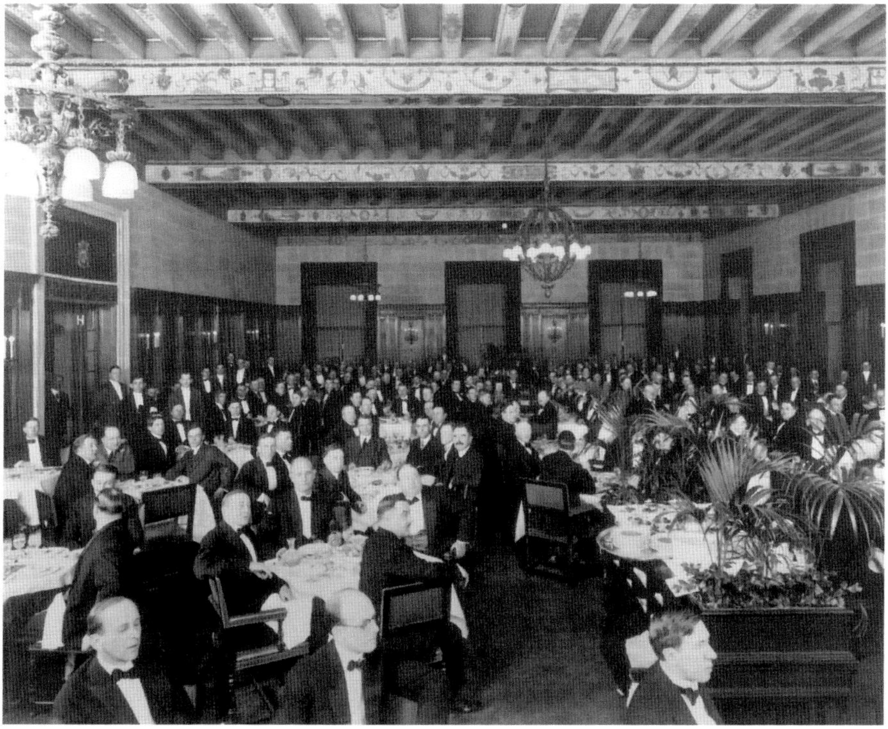

Opening week festivities in the new Main Dining Room (note the beautiful ceiling). *DAC archives.*

During a six-month research project in 2004, the number of DAC members involved in the auto business was calculated using the original membership ledgers, a document from March 1915 announcing "the roster" of members and the first roster published by the *DAC News* in September 1919. The original handwritten membership entries remain a crucial source for any study of the members' background. The first volume lists names between 1913 and 1919, from member number 1, Henry Joy, to member 4,725, C.A. Guilford. Especially useful were the entries that listed a member's company.

Using these sources—as well as others at the National Automotive History Collection—the DAC was able for the first time to identify those Detroiters (and their national counterparts) who led the world's automobile manufacture. At the same time, a close look at production sources revealed that eighteen of the top twenty car builders of the day were controlled or managed by DAC members. The top ten car builders in 1915—Ford,

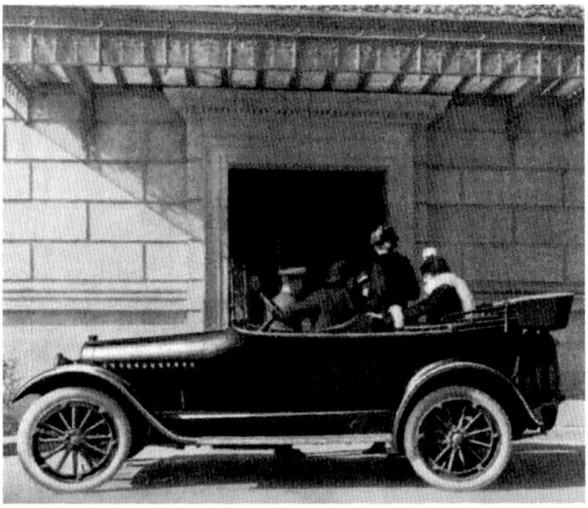

Members' wives arrive at the DAC in a Chalmers automobile. DAC News *archives.*

Willys-Overland, Buick, Dodge, Maxwell, Studebaker, Cadillac, Saxon, REO and Chevrolet—were all heavily DAC connected. Overall, of the 975,000 cars built in the United States in 1915, DAC members were responsible for just over 935,000, representing 95 percent of production.

Since World War I was raging at the time, the total world production stood that year at just over one million vehicles. By the war's end, and a return to better times in 1919, about two million cars were being built in the world—nearly 1.6 million by DAC member companies.

The DAC was at the center of this automotive whirlwind, in the world of manufacturing and technology, a revolution not unlike that which took place in Silicon Valley during the computer boom. Between 1910 and 1919, thirty-three of the top sixty car companies in the United States were DAC connected—and they were building most of the vehicles.

The top ten producers in 1919—Ford, Buick, Chevrolet, Dodge, Willys-Overland, Oakland, Maxwell, Studebaker, Oldsmobile and Nash—all had multiple memberships at the DAC. Not only was the club at the center of this dynamic new industry, but it may have also been partially responsible for it.

The club reached out into all sectors of the business. Henry Ford's huge production numbers gave the DAC auto elite a powerful advantage, but many more companies were starting to see their production numbers take off. While some of the one hundred or so automobile firms identified with DAC connections were already teetering and others had just died out before the club opened, still others were on the verge of greatness and a lasting place in American social and cultural history.

One constant, however, was the DAC itself. This new club, with its magnificent clubhouse built by Albert Kahn, represented the phoenix-like rebirth of a dying Woodward Avenue athletic club created in 1887 that lasted into early twentieth-century America to become a dynamic part of Detroit's cultural fabric.

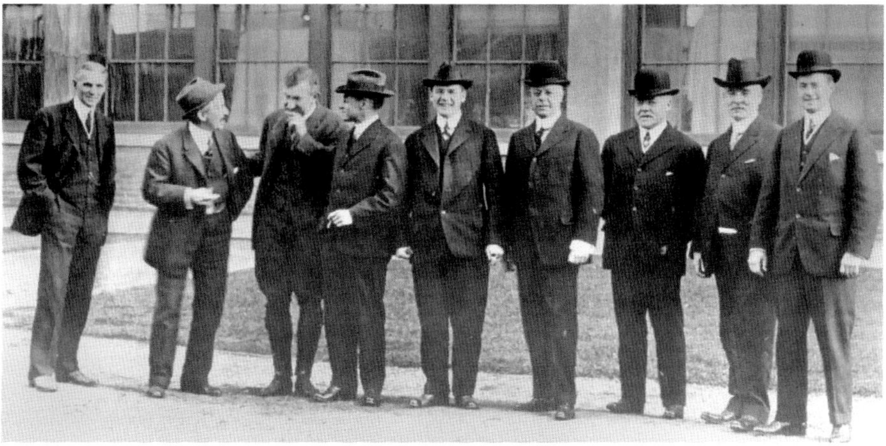

National Association of Auto Manufacturers in 1912, all DAC members. Henry Ford is at left. *National Automotive History Collection, Detroit Public Library.*

In the early years of the industry, people were moving from one company to another and the chairman of one company worked his way up with another company first, moving on and around. The place where leaders went to socialize with all these people, to make their connections and make their business, was the DAC. Indeed, the DAC was a great catalyst for bringing people together to generate camaraderie, not between companies but between people. Never before or since has one group of business leaders—tightly bound together through the DAC—so dominated an industry.

By 1912–13, it was finally becoming obvious that people everywhere were going to drive cars and the industry itself was settling down. It was now an established fact, and no one thought it was going to go away.

Besides the transformation of whole industries, the automobile itself was changing. Standardization—in production and equipment—helped drive these changes. By 1914, Henry Ford was paying his employees enough money to help them purchase the vehicles they were building. A balanced crankshaft in 1915 helped engines run twice as fast, adding horsepower and muscle to cars.

Between 1913 and 1919, the auto went from a glorified horseless carriage to something we could recognize today. The fast-growing industry was helped by a petroleum industry that found a market for gasoline and a lack of government regulations. A forgotten battle between the gasoline, steam and electric engine had just ended with a clear-cut victory for gas as the motive power in automobiles.

That's when Detroit started to take off. By 1920, the family car was a common thing, and vehicles were becoming more utilitarian. Even the predominant colors of the cars of the era showed this, with some historians labeling this the "black period," when brass trim disappeared and cars were painted dark colors.

By this time, the automobile had penetrated nearly every continent, and a whole new infrastructure was developing in support of the automobile. This, too, helped to transform the nation. Besides the engineers and builders, there were financers, publicity hounds, tinkerers and more. They were seeking ways to create products that increased individual mobility and generated skills and wealth—an undefined idea that may have been a core motivation of the early DAC pioneers.

"They had a sense of adventure," said Kimes. "It was a brave new world they were creating. Every inventor is a curious type, they are driven by an intellectual curiosity, the idea of whether he can make this thing run. Ford was most obsessed of all with the idea of creating a new world."

They were also risk takers who truly saw that this was the beginning of a whole new industry, and they wanted in on it.

In Detroit, people like Charles King, Ford, Ransom Olds, the Dodge brothers, Charles Nash, Billy Durant, David Buick, Benjamin Briscoe, Henry Joy, Roy Chapin, Hugh Chalmers and William Metzger were an odd

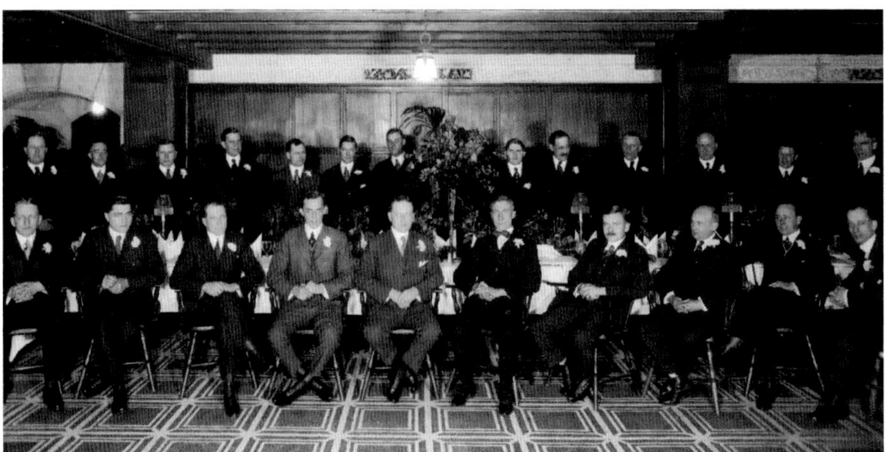

Hudson Motors executives meet in the DAC's Abbey restaurant in 1917. *Jack Miller, Ypsilanti Automotive Heritage Museum.*

mixture of old and new money, of risk takers, tinkerers and forward-thinking marketing visionaries. Clearly, then, there was a confluence of men who felt they could either build it, solve it, join it or move to it from what they were already nearly doing.

Ford, Olds, Henry Leland, Walter Flanders, Howard Coffin, Walter Chrysler, Nash and the Dodges clearly possessed outstanding manufacturing talent. These men paid close attention to design, materials and factory operations; they led by example, and others wanted to emulate them.

The risks were not as great by 1912 for those wanting to get into this "next big thing," but it was such a fluid era that anything could happen—and things like World War I certainly caught Europe and the world by surprise, opening the chance for the United States to gain dominance in world production. At first, Detroit was not the hotbed where the U.S. auto industry forged ahead. Ohio, Indiana and New York could claim large auto manufacturing centers as well, but Michigan's great resources, location and existing manufacturing base (stoves, rail cars, shipping) gave it a key advantage. Another advantage was the city's "old money," some of the men who started the transportation industry and built a club for their sons on Woodward Avenue called the Detroit Athletic Club.

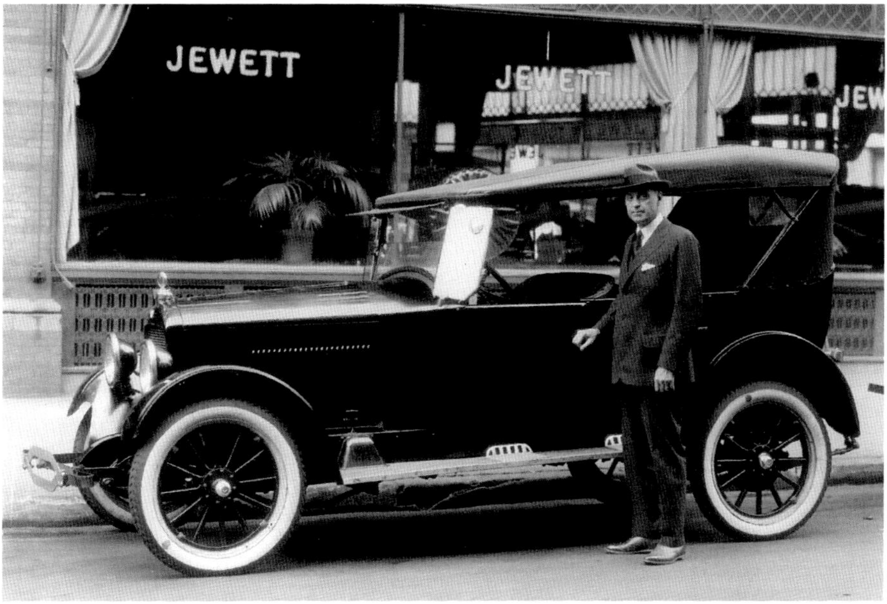

Early DAC star athlete Harry Jewett later manufactured automobiles. *National Automotive History Collection, Detroit Public Library.*

More important than a tradition of manufacturing, more important than wealth and location, however, was the very fact of the initial successes by a large number of Michigan auto builders. Successful companies like Ford, Buick, Olds, Cadillac, Packard and others led the field as early as 1907, and they were led by DAC visionaries.

In the 1928 book *A Financial History of the American Automobile Industry* by Lawrence Seltzer, the DAC's own Roy Chapin (of Hudson Motor Car Company) was quoted as saying, "Three men, Henry Ford, Ransom Olds and Charles King [all DAC members] were responsible for the origin and development of Detroit…as the center of the automobile industry. The cars they made and the companies they established were successful, while many of those made in other cities were not." Chapin added that Detroit also had skilled labor and that Michigan bankers were more willing than those on the East Coast to invest in the industry. There were more auto pioneers per capita in Detroit than any other place in the country.

As more companies developed in Detroit, it became a snowball effect; more car builders meant more machine shops, more suppliers and more people getting involved. Before his death, noted Detroit automotive journalist Richard Wright said that the presence of machine shops like those of Leland and the Dodge brothers ensured that Detroit would become an automotive center.

Detroit attracted entrepreneurs, big and small. The city was a hothouse for the new industry, and as Detroit picked up steam, it attracted brilliant people. They were drawn or sent to Detroit, with people like Ford and, later, Alfred P. Sloan relying heavily on smaller outside companies to put their vehicles together at first. The idea of assembling autos from a wide range of parts helped keep those wide-ranging businesses going strong in 1915.

The prospect of great wealth drove many of them, but the giants like Leland, Olds, Ford and others were also driven by a sense of immortality that creating a great industry might provide. Great success and great failure met these men and their companies head on.

Between 1913 and 1919, Detroit saw the formation of seventy-one new companies, while another eighty-three firms folded. Besides top producers like Olds, Packard, Brush, EMF, Hupmobile, Studebaker, GM, Hudson, Saxon, Cadillac, Chalmers, Maxwell, Dodge and Ford, many more of these DAC-connected companies would survive a few years. They included firms many barely remember: Doble, Columbia, RCH, Grinnell, Warren, Krit, Regal, Pungs-Finch, Liberty, Grant, King, Carharrt, Paige-Detroit, Abbott and Northern.

Of the top thirty-three DAC-connected auto companies in 1915, only nine failed to produce vehicles the year the club opened. Some had already ceased operation, like Brush and Detroit Electric; others, such as Harroun, Scripps-Booth and Nash, would gear up within one to two years.

While historical production (and sales) numbers tend to vary from source to source, information can be found in sources from the National Automobile Chamber of Commerce, *Automotive News*, *Commerce Yearbook* and the Automobile Manufacturers Association.

In 1915, the top ten DAC auto companies alone produced 845,000 of the nation's 975,000 cars. Of the top ten companies, Ford was far and above all others with 501,000 vehicles. Willys-Overland was next with 91,000 vehicles, and then came Buick with 57,000 and Dodge with 45,000. Only two of the top twenty were not connected to the DAC, and they built fewer than 20,000 cars combined. Other top DAC producers that year included Hudson, Oakland, Hupmobile, Chalmers, Paige, Olds, Peerless, Packard, Pierce-Arrow, King, Regal, Winton, Grant and Stutz.

Between 1913 and 1915, only three companies changed on the list of top ten firms—Hupmobile, Regal and Oakland made the list in 1913 but were no longer at the top in 1915. Oakland was back on the list by 1919 in the sixth position, and a newcomer, Nash, was tenth.

By 1915, Detroit had expanded to slightly over 50 square miles and could boast of over 528 miles of paved streets. The city's population had reached 821,000, jumping the city to fifth nationally. And it was the automobile that drove the city's growing national status.

In his history of Detroit, *All Our Yesterdays*, Arthur Woodford writes:

> *Those were exciting days in Detroit…people thought and talked about automobiles. Everyone was an expert. Groups gathered at the curb and hotly discussed the merits or faults of whatever car happened to be parked there…Millionaires less than a decade from the lathes and grinders, with the grime of the machine shops still under their fingernails, wheeled and dealed in the Pontchartrain bar or later at the DAC.*

The stories of the auto deals and the men from the industry meeting in the Pontchartrain bar have a fanciful air about them, but clearly something was going on; the leaders of this new industry came together to exchange ideas and make deals. In his 1943 book *City of Destiny*, George Stark wrote that the Pontchartrain bar was a "great workroom…it was laboratory and counting house combined. It was the cradle of a great industry."

A 1988 book, *Conspicuous Production: Automobiles and Elites in Detroit* by Donald Davis, explains that certain elements of the Pontchartrain/DAC legend are correct, as several of the auto pioneers described the bar as the industry's social club before 1912. Davis said Sloan once wrote that it was "where motorcar gossip was heard first." Sloan explained that models were debuted, sketches tossed about and partnerships made and ended at the bar. DAC member LeRoy Pelletier (Studebaker) once apparently proposed inscribing the words "the heart of the auto industry" on the floor of the Pontchartrain bar.

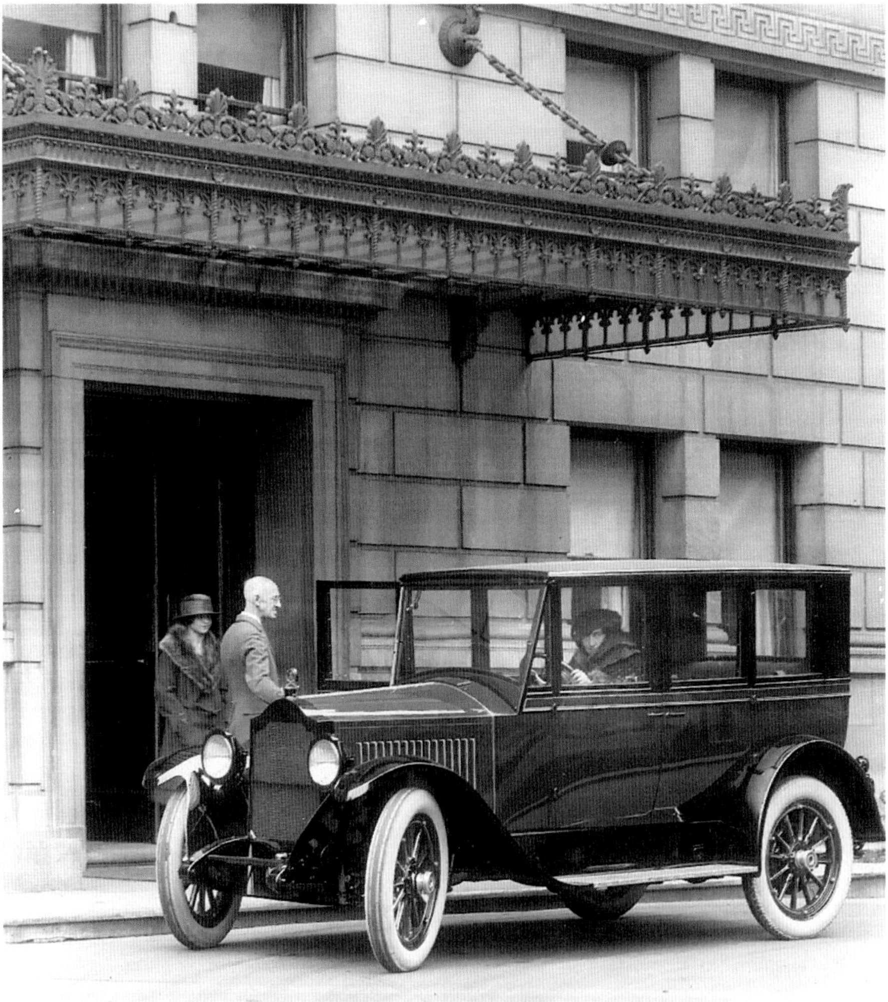

Arriving at the DAC's Randolph entrance by auto. *DAC archives.*

In this atmosphere, people like Charlie Hughes and Henry Joy came along and helped lead the auto elite from the bar into a private club, gathering a first group to discuss the idea in the very same Pontchartrain Hotel.

Historian Stark, who was also a DAC member and president of the Detroit Historical Society in 1946, ends a long description about the original Woodward DAC by explaining that the men of that club moved from youthful athletic interests into business careers—many automobile-centered. The book adds, "The men who were the star athletes then became the business, industrial and civic leaders of the town. Those of them still living will always insist that it was the Detroit Athletic Club, now occupying its handsome home on Madison Avenue, that put Detroit on the map."

Seven of the first eleven DAC presidents were automotive men, while ten of the eighteen carefully selected members of the club's first board of directors were actively engaged in the business.

Malcolm Bingay, in his 1946 book *Detroit Is My Own Hometown*, wrote that as the city was reborn under the impact of "motorcar dynamics," so was the "slumbering DAC." It was also Bingay who pointed out that many "innocents" of the day thought the DAC meant Detroit Automobile Club, "having no idea that the A meant athletics."

Originally, this new DAC wasn't considered the elite club of the city; William Metzger himself said that the club's "spontaneous success" was more due to the "salesmanship" of its organizers than prestige. Within a decade of its founding, though, the DAC had undoubtedly become the city's premier club and center for community leaders.

The DAC offered a great center for network building, pulling in more and more auto leaders from Michigan, the Midwest and the nation. It was a place of neutral ground back when auto guys hung together more than today. Developing networks, building relationships and easily arranging deals with clients allowed the auto companies to expand their reach into all parts of the city and country.

In his book *Conspicuous Production*, Davis includes a chart based on the important source *The Book of Detroiters*, which shows that the DAC was made up of 32 percent of what he calls the "auto elite." Other research suggests that the percentage of members in the auto business ranged from 20 to 25 percent throughout the 1913–19 time span.

All of this raises a tantalizing question—would Detroit have become the Motor City without the Detroit Athletic Club? It's a fascinating, albeit controversial, idea but not as far-fetched as it may seem. There's plenty of evidence to show that the members of the DAC controlled the world's car production and sales from 1913 to 1919, and these members were an important and large percentage of an industry still taking shape in Detroit and the country. Without the DAC as a place of neutral yet creative ground, there's no telling if the players would have joined so many competing companies, financed as many operations as they did or tried new (and successful) ventures, dramatically expanding the industry and outpacing the rest of the nation.

It was a vision of the future often seen by the DAC's auto giants—Ford, Olds, Hupp, Flanders, Metzger, Everitt, Leland, Dodge, Chevrolet, Chapin, Chalmers, Joy, Durant, Dort, Briscoe, Herring, Grant, Nash, Chrysler, Jewett, Handley, Grinnell, Drake, Little, Sloan, Kettering, Mott, Erskine, Brush, Briggs and many more. Beyond the twenty or thirty names on everyone's tongues even to this day, there remains an unheralded group of over seven hundred DAC members who changed the world by controlling the industry that would have the greatest impact on society until the computer industry came along seventy years later.

It is essential, then, to add another key ingredient to the birth of Detroit as "the Motor City": the Detroit Athletic Club. The DAC provided a place where auto leaders would share big ideas and small, where they could problem solve and reenergize and where they could plan an amazing future. In the end, the DAC and its leaders gave the world mobility.

Chapter 12

CLUB FLOURISHES DESPITE PROHIBITION

Detroit's economy soared in the 1920s, jazz music and the Charleston took flight, the Big Three dominated roads and the DAC flourished despite Prohibition. The dry spell began in Michigan in May 1918, when the state's amendment banning the sale and manufacture of alcohol took effect. Like all public places, the club was obligated to end the drinking and sale of booze and made its official stance by establishing House Rule No. 44: "The bringing of liquor into the dining rooms or locker rooms is prohibited."

The question was brought up on numerous occasions, causing manager Walter S. Cummings to instruct that all staff "report and stop the use of alcoholic beverages." Any employee seen supplying alcohol would be discharged. Dr. James Inches, a Detroit police commissioner and DAC director, recommended that all liquor be removed from members' lockers. Yet there is a sense that turning a blind eye to private gatherings in the rooms on the upper floors was common. Apparently, even Commissioner Inches was one among many who might have done so.

Proof of a somewhat wet clubhouse comes from the claim that a 1920s cocktail enjoying a recent resurgence at trendy nightclubs originated at the DAC. With the creation of the green chartreuse and maraschino–infused "Last Word" attributed to the DAC, it's unclear how dry the club really was.

The Volstead Act, America's Eighteenth Amendment, intended to sober up the country, had unwanted consequences, including a rise in organized crime and speakeasies. With Canada less than a mile away across the Detroit River, the city became a hotspot for smuggling. Along with Lake St. Clair and the St. Clair River, the waterways around Detroit accounted for about 75 percent of liquor smuggled into the United States in the dry years.

DAC member Hiram H. Walker, grandson of the famed American distiller Hiram Walker, had a direct hand in the business. After his grandfather died in 1899, he ran the family's whiskey business in Windsor for nearly thirty years. The popularity of "gentlemen's clubs" in the United States and Canada gave Walker's whiskey its name: Canadian Club.

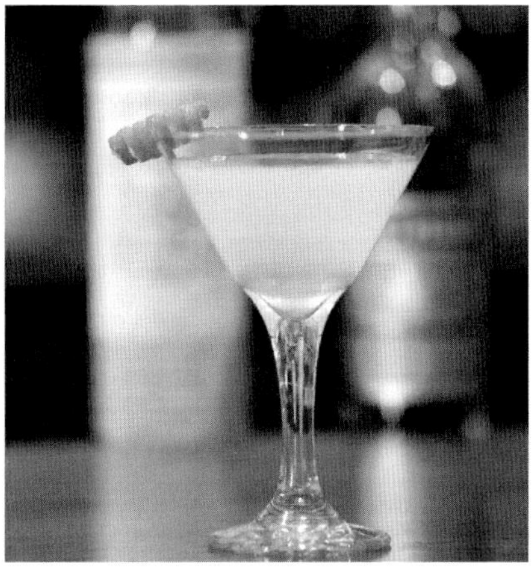

The Last Word, a drink created at the DAC sometime during the 1920s or later. DAC News *image.*

Walker made deals with Chicago's Al Capone and helped make smuggling easier. To keep the tall necks of bottles from breaking, Canadian Club created the "bootlegger's" bottle, flat with a short neck easily concealed in pockets or boots.

As 1920 came to an end, the club prepared for its New Year's Eve party, and one question continued to be asked by members: "May I bring something on the hip?" The house committee announced that fun could be had without champagne. Yet the guest rooms very easily could have become a place to ring in the New Year with spirits.

Enjoying cocktails in the guest rooms became a common Prohibition activity. In fact, the prince of Wales, Edward Albert, was a guest of Edsel Ford in 1924 and was put up in one of the rooms. During his stay, the prince received a "lesson" from club member Phelps Newberry on mixing cocktails in Commissioner Inches's room.

The *DAC News* published several stories of rumrunning in the 1920s, some quite humorous. But tales of bootleggers were often filled with crime and mayhem. Hijacking hooch was the modus operandi for Detroit's notorious Purple Gang. Bootleggers needed to be alert, prepared and use caution along the Detroit River. It was public knowledge that "the Purples" would hijack the liquor and get rid of anyone who was with it.

The Purples maintained control of the Detroit underworld during the 1920s and early '30s, bribing police, judges and politicians. When they weren't running liquor, the gang took part in other criminal activity. In 1929, the infamous Valentine's Day Massacre took place in Chicago, and the

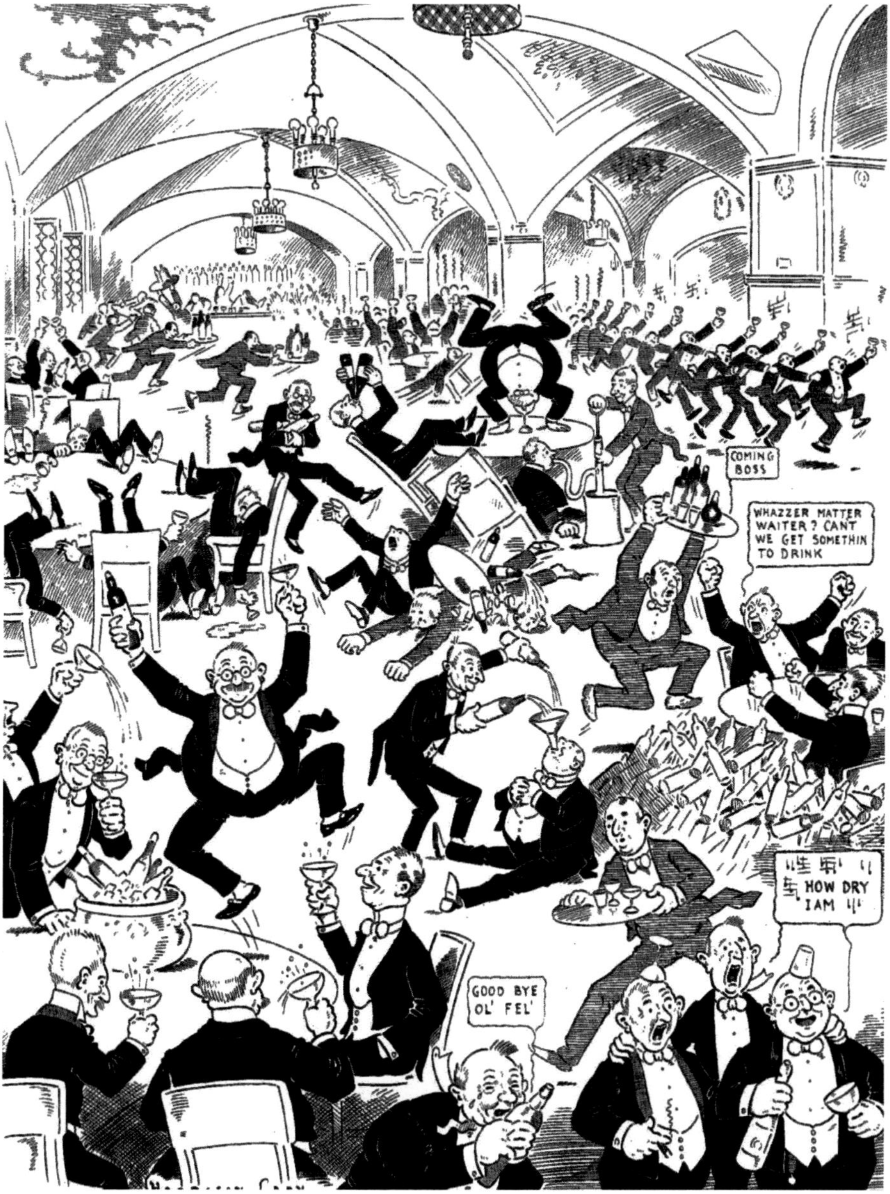

A *DAC News* cartoon lampoons Prohibition. DAC News *archives.*

execution of three Purples by fellow gang members followed in 1931. The inter-gang execution became known as the Collingwood Massacre, which ultimately led to the gang's demise in 1935.

By 1928, the Detroit Board of Commerce had declared that liquor was the city's second largest industry, generating $215 million in sales, second only to auto manufacturing.

Club member Henry Ford's automobile company had been founded well before the 1920s and grew rapidly in that era. The Model A debuted in 1927, the company expanded internationally and Ford opened the Henry Ford Museum in 1929, standing alongside Thomas Edison and President Hoover.

Competition in Detroit began to grow, with General Motors taking what would be its final form for the remainder of the twentieth century. DAC member and founder of GM William C. Durant left the company for good in late 1920. GM's new leadership—Pierre S. du Pont and DAC members Alfred P. Sloan Jr. and William S. Knudsen—helped revive the company and the Chevrolet division. Becoming more competitive, GM added Pontiac and the LaSalle to the production line.

Chrysler gained momentum during the Prohibition era, when Walter P. Chrysler, the founder and a DAC member, bought the Dodge Brothers. Chrysler was the last of the Big Three to roll out its first automobile in 1924, but with the purchase of Dodge Brothers in 1928, the company secured its place among Detroit automakers.

Successful and innovative automakers John and Horace Dodge were DAC members known for throwing lavish parties where money was no object to having a good time. Despite their untimely deaths in 1920, the Dodges remain a valuable part of Detroit's automobile history.

The *DAC News* featured humorous cartoons and advertisements alluding to Prohibition—along with a blatant advertisement for Budweiser beer in a 1924 issue.

When the club celebrated its tenth anniversary in 1925, membership exceeded the limit of 2,500. To bring the number back within DAC bylaws, directors began electing only one new member for every two vacancies. The wait list grew to more than 1,000 hopefuls.

It was first proposed in 1926 to build an expansion to the clubhouse or to purchase an adjacent property, but two past DAC presidents, John Kelsey and Abner Larned, fought hard against this, and members voted it down. Three years later, the stock market crashed, and Kelsey and Larned were credited with doing the club a great deed.

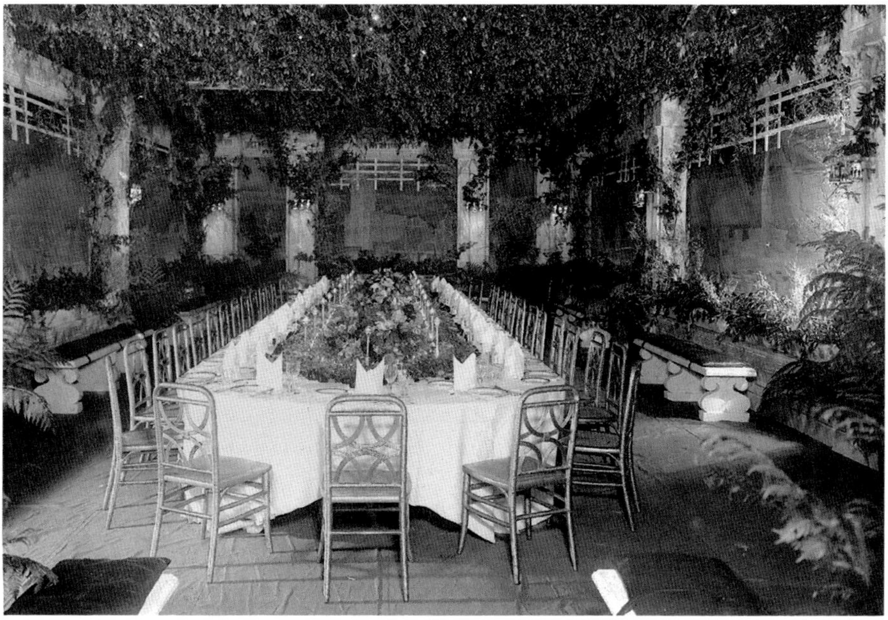

Lavish parties were the order of the day in the 1920s, despite Prohibition. *DAC archives.*

During the 1920s, the city's population swelled by more than 500,000, putting Detroit over the 1.5 million mark by 1930. Breathtaking skyscrapers appeared downtown, including the Guardian, Stott and Penobscot buildings. The Fox, the Michigan and the Fisher were opulent new theaters.

With travel to Windsor at an all-time high, the opening of the Ambassador Bridge in 1929, followed by the Detroit Windsor Tunnel in 1930, was greatly welcomed.

Prohibition did cause the club financial losses because alcohol was not served openly, leading members who wanted a beer with their steak to opt for dinner at one of Detroit's twenty-five thousand speakeasies. One force that helped the crowds return for supper was the red-hot jazz of DAC music director Jean Goldkette presiding over the first original white swing band in history. In 1926, his orchestra included Tommy and Jimmy Dorsey, cornetist Bix Beiderbecke and Hoagy Carmichael. In addition to his regular gig at the DAC, Goldkette co-owned Detroit's Graystone Ballroom and ran an entertainment business from the Book Cadillac Hotel.

Internationally known entertainers kept the DAC gym full in the spring of 1924, when magician Harry Houdini and American monologist

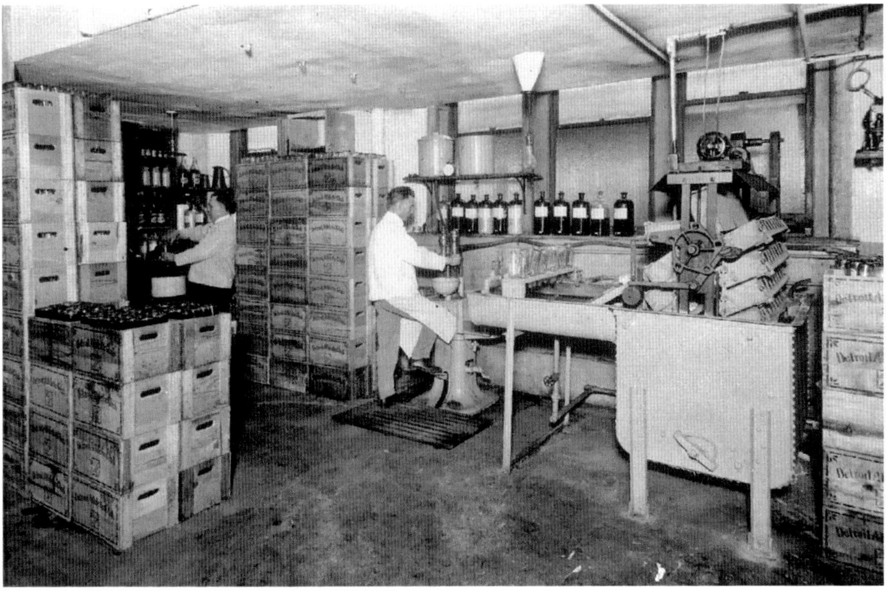

A DAC bottling operation made soft drinks, including sarsaparilla. *DAC archives.*

Ruth Draper came to town. Hundreds had to be turned away for each performance. Along with jazz, these popular shows further helped the club coffers during Prohibition.

The 1920 presidential election marked the first year women could vote, with the Nineteenth Amendment ratified the prior summer. It was also the year Helen Newberry Joy—wife of the club's third president—fought to give the wives of members a perk their husbands already enjoyed. Mrs. Joy struggled to convince the board of directors to allow women to smoke inside the clubhouse. Patient and gaining support from the other wives, Joy's persistence paid off when the proposal came to a vote in 1924, only to be denied. Despite losing, women defied the ban, and the rule was ignored by all, putting an end to a four-year argument.

The Roaring Twenties came to an abrupt halt with the stock market crash on October 29, 1929. Prohibition would continue for four more years until April 1933, when Americans could again drink freely. Hughes figured the ban had cost the DAC $2.5 million over fifteen years in lost revenue. On the night of repeal, DAC revelers quaffed six thousand glasses of good beer, jamming the first two floors of the clubhouse and spilling into the lounge and billiards room. The clubhouse was filled with "more smiles and heartier laughter" than it had seen in years.

Chapter 13

CHARLIE HUGHES AND THE *DAC NEWS*

What began as a ninety-day trial reached a ninety-five-year legacy in 2011. First published in January 1916, the *DAC News* magazine's unbroken publishing track record speaks volumes about its founder, Charles A. Hughes, and all those who carried on the publication and have been responsible for the great success of what is today Michigan's oldest continuously published monthly magazine.

The early dream of Hughes—affectionately known as "Mr. DAC" for his role in creating the downtown Detroit Athletic Club—was to produce the finest publication, let alone a club publication, in the country. And indeed he did, serving as publisher, editor and chief booster for thirty-seven years while running the club as its first secretary and executive manager.

Over the magazine's lifespan, DAC members have witnessed a publication that never let them down and that arrived every month, through the jazz age, the Great Depression, two world wars, postwar auto and baby booms and the bitter economic challenges of the 1970s and '80s.

The *DAC News* magazine was conceived of by Hughes in the fall of 1915, presented to the DAC Board of Directors in October of that year and born with the release of the first issue in January 1916—all less than a year after the club opened on Madison Avenue. It was a time of growing popularity for magazines across the country. Americans were gobbling up portable reading material, often including some of the best in American fiction and art. Many new publications were finding niches, but the days of *Time*, *Life* and the *New Yorker* still lay ahead.

With no prior experience putting together a magazine, Hughes's proposal to the board smacked of grandstanding, especially considering that the time between the board's tentative okay of the concept and the birth of the magazine was identical to that given for the trial publication period—three months. A remarkable job, no doubt, pulling together a brand-new magazine out of thin air and hitting the "newsstands" of the DAC before members realized what was happening.

The *DAC News* and the DAC career of Charlie Hughes came into being simultaneously, the one a corollary of the other. His task as club organizational secretary was at an end when the DAC opened in April 1915. He was presented with a year's salary as a bonus, with the gratitude of the DAC Board of Directors.

Hughes was apparently out of a job and could have easily left the DAC to return to the world of advertising he already knew so well (he was a president of the Adcraft Club and a former PR director for Hudson Motors). Instead, he went on to found what Clarence Burton, Detroit's renowned historian, called one of the "most distinctive club magazines in the country."

With extraordinary insight into the future of the institution he helped plan and build, Hughes proposed that he serve as unpaid secretary of the new club in return for the franchise of publishing its own magazine. Hughes's purpose, according to his daughter Harriet Hughes Crowley (a writer for the *DAC News* in the 1950s) was simply to bring the best, most entertaining writers in the country under one cover. In the process, several writers who became among the country's most famous were published in the *DAC News* before they appeared in any other magazine.

It appears that the directors' response to Hughes's idea was less than enthusiastic. Eddie A. Batchelor, Hughes's longtime partner at the *DAC News* and a renowned sportswriter, later said that the club was "neither asked to underwrite the magazine nor to advance any money for its establishment and operation." Batchelor said Hughes planned to "do all the gambling on the success or failure of the proposed publication, and he staked all the money he had in the world that he could make it a winner."

As the story goes, the magazine would serve the purpose as a clubhouse "organ" but also be a magazine that was read with interest by people who did not even know what the initials DAC stood for.

In exchange for the franchise, Hughes developed the *DAC News* into a property that greatly added to the prestige of the club, yielding returns the directors could never have imagined.

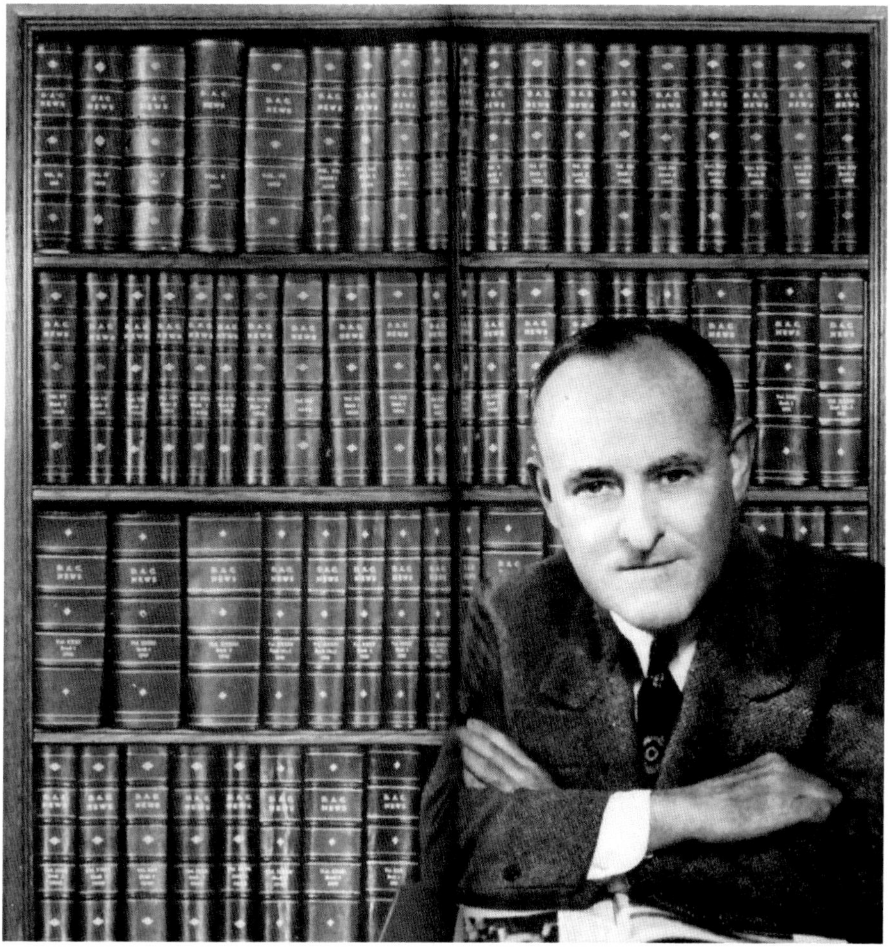

Charlie Hughes with bound volumes of the *DAC News*. DAC News *archives*.

According to what may be Hughes's only direct account of the magazine's creation, the DAC Board met on October 15, 1915, to discuss publishing a club magazine. Obviously, the idea had already been set in motion, and Hughes was looking for agreement from the directors. And he got it as Bill Metzger made the motion to "get out a club magazine on three months trial." The account adds just a hint of sly editorialization for history with the following line: "'It better be good,' was the pointed hint from the board members."

As Hughes moved from planning to executing his vision, he turned to a baseball writer he knew from his newspaper days in Chicago. Ring Lardner was a native of Niles, Michigan, and is most famous today for his humorous baseball stories, especially "You Know Me, Al." At the time, Lardner was a columnist for the *Chicago Tribune*, but when Hughes asked if he wanted to be the managing editor for a new magazine, the young reporter accepted. Little did Hughes know that Lardner was about to hit the national scene with his first short story published in the *Saturday Evening Post*. Once Hughes saw the piece, he realized that Lardner was destined to write and not be his managing editor. Hughes championed his cause, and Lardner ended up writing stories for the *DAC News* in the form of letters to "Dear Chas." He never did take a turn as a DAC editor.

So without a full-time managing editor, Hughes plowed forward, and on New Year's Day 1916, the *DAC News* was born. The cover showed the clubhouse's front door on Madison Avenue. For the issue, John C. Lodge related the history of the original DAC. Other features included poems from Grantland Rice and Edgar A. Guest and a column by president Hugh Chalmers urging members to protect the club's "good name with the same zeal and dignity that are expected of us in guarding our own firesides."

Henry B. Joy, later the club's third president and a stalwart athletic member of the first club, secured the first advertisement for the magazine from the National Bank of Commerce. He also made sure that his own Packard Motor Company was in with a marvelous "greetings" to members, noting that the twenty-nine Packard members were grateful for the club's "spirit of mutual respect and goodwill." Among the other major advertisers in that first issue were Chalmers, Hudson, Hupp, Maxwell, Firestone, Anderson Electric, Studebaker, Goebel and Pfeiffer beers.

While he was publishing the magazine on behalf of the DAC, Hughes did not have a contract with the club, and it appears he had not yet incorporated his publication. In August 1916, the DAC board called a special meeting solely to consider the one-dollar charge per year for the club magazine. Charter member Judge George P. Codd was authorized to make a contract with Hughes for publishing the magazine in the ensuing year.

By December 1916, the DAC board was ready to sign a contract with Hughes. By this document, it becomes clear that the time had come to truly turn over the *DAC News* to Hughes so that the club could get out of the publishing business. In the approved agreement, Hughes was given a one-year contract, subject to renewal each year.

After less than a year, Hughes had secured the magazine's future. He would move forward right away to incorporate the *DAC News* under his name and take complete control. At the same time, he remained essentially in charge of the clubhouse, putting in practice the policies and desires of the board of directors.

By March, Hughes, still without a managing editor, had turned to noted Detroit historian and DAC member George Stark as his regular associate editor. In a March issue, Hughes notes that the magazine had been receiving both "bouquets and brickbats" but that, happily, there had been more bouquets for the magazine than the latter. Hughes called his magazine a "family magazine" that might lack "flash" but was now clearly an established institution.

By October 1917, the *DAC News* was receiving mail from members who were in France during World War I. One such member, Lieutenant Ray Middleton, actually claimed that he walked into a bookstore in France and asked for the *DAC News*. Undeterred by his inability to find the magazine in France, Middleton wrote to Hughes asking for copies to be mailed to him so that he may "feel nearer home." He added that he never realized what a "newsy little sheet the *News* was before" and missed it terribly.

During the war, the magazine published a tribute on the cover of the December 1917 issue showing a special servicemen's flag with stars representing the members in action. This was the first full-color cover of the magazine.

In December 1918, a full-color painting appeared on the cover. This Christmas scene was by local artist R.F. Heinrich, one of a group of commercial artists organized as the Advertiser's Bureau, whose staff acted as art editors for the *DAC News* for forty years.

The Bureau's Thomas M. Neilson was art editor from 1916 to 1922, at which point a young man named Joseph C. Faust, destined to guide the magazine's art and makeup policy as art director for nearly four decades, was appointed. Other regular artists included cartoonist Burt Thomas and illustrator Russell Legge. But it was Heinrich who created more than sixty original covers between June 1919 and November 1924. A master of woodcut illustration, his works focused on Detroit sports activities and teams but also included holiday and nature scenes.

With the style of the magazine demanding a great deal of illustrations, cartoons and drawings to accompany the writing, Legge and Thomas were critical members of the staff. Thomas's cartoons also appeared in the *Detroit News*.

By September 1919, the *DAC News* was ready to publish the club's first "yearbook," today known as "the Roster." This revolutionary undertaking apparently took more than two years to pull off, interrupted at one point by the city's realigning its street numbering system, throwing address directories into temporary chaos. Further yearbooks would be published every other year until 1927, when the Roster would become an annual project.

The war and the advent of Prohibition kept Secretary Hughes busy, but Publisher Hughes found time to do most of the editorial writing for the first year or two. Then the masthead began to swell with names listed as assistant editors, a courtesy title for its contributors.

Besides his role as sometime associate editor, George Stark, often called the official historiographer of Detroit, supplied humor and nostalgia. Poets Edgar Guest and Grantland Rice added to the editorial makeup of the magazine. Humorist Al Weeks also supplied occasional pieces. Another key player was Eddie "Batch" Batchelor, who remained with the *DAC News* until his death in 1968. Batchelor had his own career at the *Free Press* but was Hughes's right-hand man and friend for many years.

As the 1920s began, the magazine started to flex its muscles and expand, including work by *Life* managing editor Thomas L. Masson and Canadian humorist Stephen Leacock.

In a small item in the October 1920 issue, an important turn of events was announced. Under the headline "Star Writers Signed," Hughes told members that Ring Lardner would be sending in contributions to the magazine, as would the drama critic for *Life*, Robert Benchley, well known for his *Vanity Fair* stories. While Lardner used his comic genius in more than 60 pieces, Benchley, another outstanding American humorist, would write a column on theater, humor or travel for the magazine. He would become renowned at the DAC for essays later in the 1920s when he satirized the founding of the club and the creation of the first Roster. Thanks to people like Benchley, the magazine began to take on a distinct personality and to take advantage of one of the greatest

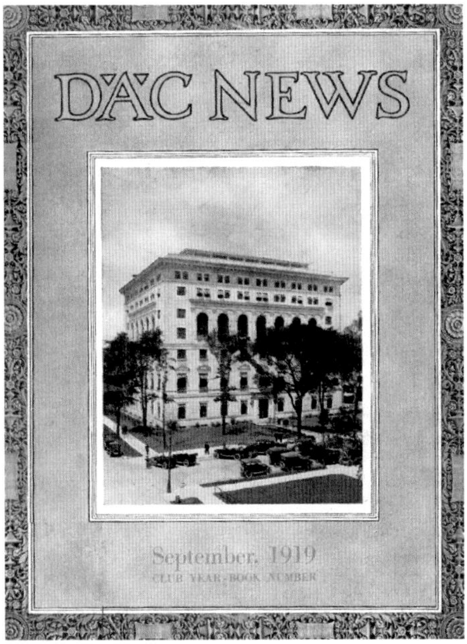

The cover of the first *DAC News* "member yearbook" in 1919. DAC News *archives*.

eras of humor this country has ever known. The *DAC News* published Benchley's stories regularly—about 128 in all—until the mid-1930s. Many of Benchley's pals also became contributors, such as nationally known author Dorothy Parker, who first appeared in the *DAC News* with a lighthearted piece in the September 1922 issue.

By 1921, DAC members had begun dubbing the *DAC News* "WGM," an acronym for "World's Greatest Magazine." In 1922, George Bernard Shaw turned down Hughes's request for three stories. He also declined to engage in a spiritualism debate in the magazine with Sherlock Holmes creator Sir Arthur Conan Doyle in 1924. Doyle appeared in the magazine in May 1924, when he wrote a letter to the *DAC News* after an article about Harry Houdini's visit to the club earlier that year. He had received a copy of "your interesting journal" from a friend and wanted to react to the information presented about Houdini's take on spiritualism.

The long list of contributors to the *DAC News* reads like a catalogue of famous American writers. There was the "Indiana sage," George Ade. There were humorists Gelette Burgess, Strickland Gillilan, Kyle Crichton, Corey Ford, Leacock, Parker and even the famed British writer P.G. Wodehouse, who appeared in 1926. Ben Hecht and O.O. McIntrye, Walter Winchell and Alexander Woolcott also added their voices to Hughes's publication.

There was an impressive list of cartoonists and illustrators as well. Many of the early ones—Don Herold, Rube Goldberg, H.T. Webster, *Vanity Fair* caricaturist Gluyas Williams and *Vanity Fair* illustrator Ralph Barton—were personal friends Hughes had met at the regular Artists and Writers Association dinners in New York. But it was the reputation of the magazine itself that attracted such later contributors as Syd Hoff, Al Hirschfeld, Rea Irvin, Virgil Partch, Gardner Rea, Barney Tobey and Mischa Richter. One of Hughes's major catches was the illustration work of John Held Jr., whose satirical flapper sketches delighted readers in nearly every issue. Held submitting drawings into the 1930s.

One of the great moments in this golden era occurred with the publication in November 1925 of an unknown writer and artist named James Thurber. This was to be Thurber's first published magazine piece, entitled "Quick, the Other Side!" Thurber had landed a job with the Paris edition of the *Chicago Tribune*, and Hughes had apparently never heard of him when the story arrived in the mail. Hughes bought the piece, which was about the difficulties of train travel in France. Hughes's daughter, Harriet, later said it was quite likely her father "never knew" he was the first magazine editor to publish Thurber, who was down on his luck and ready to give up his lackluster literary career. She said in the 1950s that Thurber retained a "soft spot in his heart for the *DAC News* because it had given his luck a 180-degree turn for the better."

In the days before the fabled *New Yorker* magazine, Hughes offered a great place to be published. A New York fixture, Frank Sullivan wrote for the DAC for thirty years. He said that Hughes was a constant presence in New York at the annual Dutch Treat Club dinners, a group of literary and theater types that also included Harold Ross, founder of the *New Yorker*. Sullivan recalled Hughes as a charter member of "the Table," a sub-group of the Dutch Treat Club, along with Ross, Corey Ford and Russell Crouse. Through this group, Hughes got to know many of the literary agents and their artists; he would even bring other members of the magazine staff, likely Batchelor. Eventually, he was nearly as well known in New York as in Detroit.

Humorist Weare Holbrook first met Hughes at the Dutch Treat Club before becoming a monthly contributor. Later on, the magazine published works by Paul Gallico, Stanley Walker, S.S. Van Dine, Groucho Marx, Baird Leonard, Donald Ogden Stuart, Arthur C. Clarke, Charles Goren and British humorist C. Northcote Parkinson.

Besides the Dutch Treat Club, Hughes developed ties with the original literary club in New York, the fabled Algonquin Club, thanks in part to his ties with Ross, Benchley and other New Yorkers.

To this day, it is DAC lore that Hughes's *DAC News* influenced Harold Ross and his colleagues in the creation and eventual look of the *New Yorker*. Some point to the use of cartoons, drawings and illustrations, as well as the wealth of essays found in the original *DAC News* issues. The magazine's "Heard in the Lobby" (first appearing in 1916) may have inspired the *New Yorker*'s "Talk of the Town."

The hard work and long hours involved in putting together a magazine of such worth and complexity took its toll on Hughes, who turned to Batchelor and members of his own family to help. Daughters Harriet and Mary would both become *DAC News* correspondents. Hughes's wife, Anna Corbin Hughes, would proofread the magazine and remain one of her husband's steadfast helpers. After Hughes died, she was an important factor, and her personality was "impressed on every issue."

As the 1920s wrapped up, Baird Leonard wrote book reviews, Frank Sullivan appeared for the first time and newsy commentary came from Paris (Solita Solano), New York (Walter Winchell) and Hollywood (E.E. Paramore).

Long before swimsuit issues, the *DAC News* regularly ran a full page devoted to daintily clad Hollywood starlets, showgirls and performers. The magazine also carried its own "Our Hall of Fame" page each month, gently praising (and mocking) figures of the day.

The crash of 1929 hit Hughes a hard blow, but the magazine regained ground at the end of the 1930s, continuing to publish the likes of Held, Benchley, Groucho Marx and Lowell Thomas.

When the war broke out in 1941, Hughes faced a paper shortage for his magazine. With advertisers once more demanding space, he was hard pressed to publish issues large enough. In 1943, only eleven issues were published, as the June and July issues were combined into one copy. That issue was also the first time a cartoon appeared on the cover; it depicted a frantic Hitler shrinking in fright against a map of Europe and the bayonets of the Allies.

A year after the war ended, DAC member Malcolm Bingay published his *Detroit Is My Own Home Town* book that, in part, outlined the foundation of the new DAC. Bingay writes, "During lush years 'poor Charlie' netted as high as $50,000 a year out of his magazine, the *DAC News*. He didn't know anything about making motorcars, nor much about finance, but he did know advertising. He is still secretary without salary and the *DAC News* goes merrily along into its 30th year."

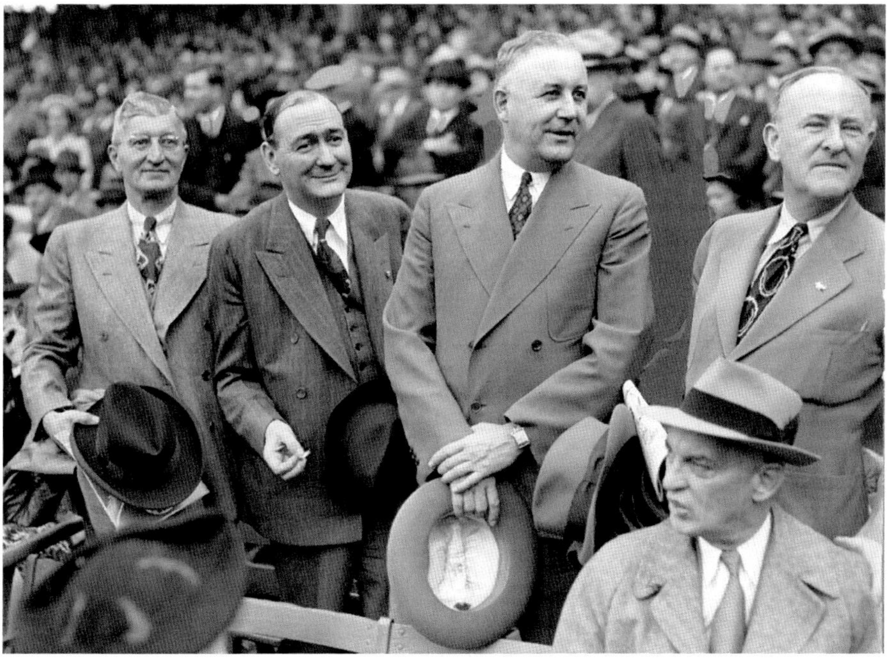

Charlie Hughes (standing right) with DAC board members at Tiger Stadium for the 1940 World Series. DAC News *archives.*

When the war ended, business in Detroit boomed, and advertising in the *DAC News* of the late 1940s once again made the book as thick as suburban telephone directories.

The club's appreciation for Hughes's service took a tangible form in May 1950, when one of the most memorable testimonial dinners in Detroit took place at the DAC. More than seven hundred members and guests filled the club for a gala evening honoring "Mr. DAC." Among the speakers were GM president Charles Wilson, Chrysler president K.T. Keller and Lincoln-Mercury president Benson Ford. Both Edgar Guest and Grantland Rice composed special poems honoring Hughes, and the club presented the publisher with a $10,000 U.S. Savings Bond, a gift from his friends.

To paraphrase Rice's poem, he noted that Detroit could do "without General Motors," "without Briggs and Chrysler," "without the Tigers," "without Walter Reuther," "without scotch, bourbon or gin," but how "could the city do without Charlie Hughes?"

Within three years of that night, the DAC and Detroit would lose Charlie Hughes. A brief obituary appeared in the February 1953 *DAC News* with a black border stating that, with infinite regret, the club had learned of the death of Charles Augustus Hughes, who died on January 29, 1953, following a cerebral thrombosis. The statement said that if an institution is but the length and shadow of a man, then the Detroit Athletic Club, "in all it is and all it stands for, is truly his monument."

Hughes had suffered a stroke on the train to Miami from the 1953 DAC annual meeting just a few days earlier. He was laid in state at the DAC for two hours—the only time such an honor has been bestowed.

But his legacy lives on through those editors who have run the magazine for the DAC ever since and the commitment by the DAC to maintain the finest club publication anywhere.

Chapter 14

SURVIVING THE DEPRESSION WITH GRIT AND DETERMINATION

Detroit was regarded by the rest of the country as a fit model for a statue of the Depression. Our wheels were scarcely turning, our population was vanishing. To be from Detroit was to evoke a mirthless joke.

Those words were penned in 1934 by *DAC News* publisher Charles Hughes as the darkest days of the Great Depression passed. Years before, though, as the country fell into an economic abyss, every segment of society was touched, even the esteemed Detroit Athletic Club. A tsunami of challenges, from declining membership to shrinking budgets to Prohibition, would test club leaders during those sobering years. Yet shepherded by some of the sharpest minds in the business community, the club would prevail.

The Roaring Twenties saw some of Detroit's finest buildings erected, automotive production in full swing, plenty of jobs and free-spending consumers. That changed with the stock market crash of October 29, 1929. Thousands lost their money in the market, spending tightened up and the boom deflated. The great reservoir of easy money and credit evaporated.

With its heavy reliance on the automobile industry, Detroit was one of the first cities to feel the fallout. Vehicle production dropped from over 5.0 million units in 1929 to just 1.3 million two years later. That led to extensive factory layoffs, which led to a more widespread cycle of economic hardship. Desperation was so encompassing that Detroit mayor Frank Murphy converted three factories into shelters for homeless men and oversaw tent colonies in local parks for evicted families. Long bread lines snaked down streets and around corners.

Inside the clubhouse, some effects of the crash were felt immediately. In November 1929, club receipts were off by $4,000—caused principally by a drop in special dinners and banquets. Yet as 1930 dawned, club members were in good hands. Among those elected to the board were the presidents of Hudson Motors, Michigan Bell, Campbell-Ewald, Michigan Mutual Insurance and the J.L. Hudson Company.

According to the president's report that year, profits from guest rooms were down $9,000 from 1929. In the first two months of 1930, the club lost $10,000. A year later, when revenue loss in January and February spiked at $4,000, Hughes deemed it "a moral victory."

The DAC maintained a healthy profile primarily due to entrance fees. While receipts from operations were $3,200 less than expenditures, funds received from entrance fees amounted to about $100,000, and this allowed several projects to go forward. An elevator was installed in the ladies' department, two squash courts were built, a linen room was added and the women's reception room was remodeled. Telephone booths and smoking stands appeared, a new lighting arrangement was configured in the card room and carpeting was laid in several rooms. Automotive tycoon and 1930 president Charles Fisher noted in his year-end report, "Whatever changes were made were of necessity, but to make them in anything but good taste would have been a needless setback for the club and its good name."

While some new blood trickled in, others were leaving the club in unprecedented numbers. Resignations reached the highest levels in the DAC's then fifteen-year history. Eighty-one resident and eighty-five nonresident members called it quits in 1930.

By year's end and $6,425 in the red, the DAC marked the first of five consecutive years of losses. Even a New Year's Eve gala for just $9 a plate didn't elicit much interest.

Soon, dwindling membership began taking a toll. In January 1931, the U.S. Census Bureau declared Detroit hardest hit of nineteen major cities. That year, ninety DAC members resigned in June alone. The board decided to put $200,000 of club reserve into U.S. Treasury bonds, a fortuitous move.

The president of the club that year was one of the most popular executives in the auto world, Hupp Motor Car president DuBois Young. With an able board of directors, the club survived another perilous year, with a loss of $43,000 due primarily to members' delinquent accounts.

In June 1932, some 128 members resigned, and nearly as many in July. Club leaders scrambled for ways to retain the faithful and attract new blood.

One promotion offered lunch in the Grill Room restaurant for fifty cents, with heartier fare for seventy-five cents.

In January 1933, outgoing DAC president Herbert Trix, president of a local automotive supplier and a former mayor of Grosse Pointe, stated that 1932 had been a very trying year. Directors had been in almost daily meetings for weeks at a sacrifice of much time and expense. The main purpose of these numerous sessions was to devise ways for meeting the distressing state of club business in order to make the burden on members as light as possible. Operations losses of $62,000, offset by entrance fees, netted the club a $43,000 loss in 1932, and Trix and his board vowed to carry on so that each member would continue to be proud of the organization.

"We could cut dues if we eliminated music and dancing," noted Trix, at forty the youngest president in club history, "if we closed the dining rooms at 9 p.m. and did away with Saturday night entertainments, the smokers, the footmen we maintain to assist members in parking, but we know that you do not want these curtailments. The club would no longer be the DAC."

The previous December, the annual Christmas fund had netted only $10,850, less than half the average workers had received from members over the past decade, but employees were grateful. The staff also took a salary cut of 10 percent in 1932.

By November, members could buy rolls of tokens from DAC clerks to dole out to panhandlers. Each chip could be redeemed for seven cents' worth of food at the Penny Pantry on Woodward Avenue.

The following year, the club loss ballooned to $155,000. More than one-third of membership went delinquent on accounts, and by March, the club did business strictly on a cash basis—achieved by selling coupon books for food and services. Some $25,000 in government bonds was sold for operating revenue.

The waiting list evaporated, and membership fizzled to 1,892 by the end of 1933—a loss of 30 percent in just three years.

The price of almost everything was lowered: room rates, meals (dinner for $1.10), the cost of a game of billiards and also bowling. Every effort was made to provide the best service to members at a lower price. Even as such adjustments were made, leaders were mindful of maintaining the club's prestigious reputation. Other clubs weren't faring as well. The Detroit Golf Club temporarily closed its doors, and the Detroit Club closed its restaurant and shuttered at night.

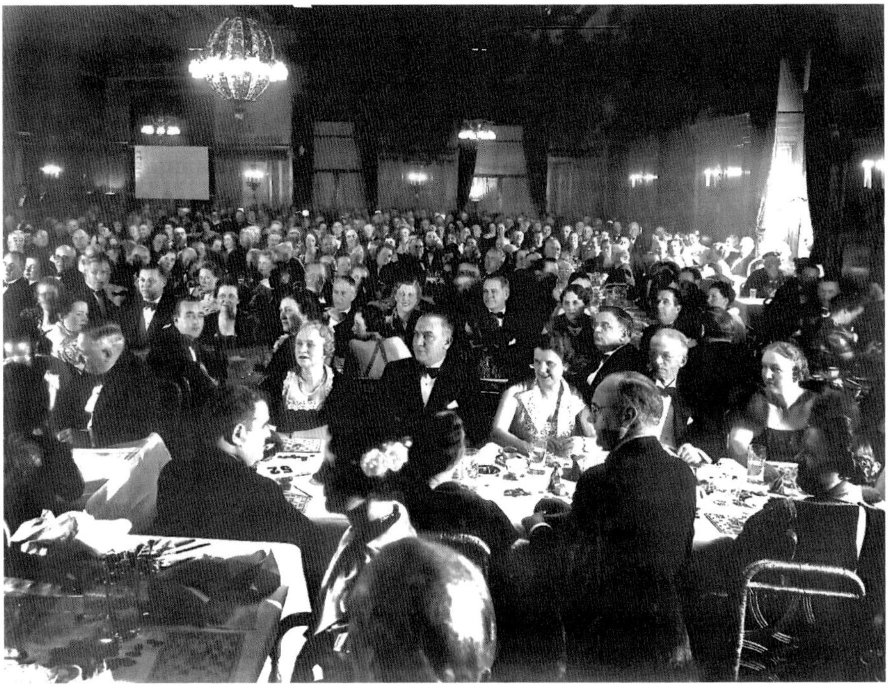

A keno party, a popular DAC pastime in the 1930s. *DAC archives.*

It was against this backdrop that DAC member Edsel Ford commissioned Mexican muralist Diego Rivera to create his now famous Industry murals at the Detroit Institute of Arts.

The *DAC News*, published monthly since 1916, never missed an issue during the Depression, although volumes were slimmer. While advertisements hawked Cadillacs, Buicks and fancy hotels, a distressing sign of the times was ads for deeply discounted Grosse Pointe estates and luxurious yachts.

As members dealt with their own financial losses, they continued to swim in the pool and lunch on Thursday with the Beavers. They played racquetball and bowled in the Abbey, where the bowling program actually grew during the Depression. Members dined on tantalizing club delicacies and packed the clubhouse to watch folk dancers or listen to classical music performances. Hughes revitalized attractions in late 1933, and soon the likes of Ed Sullivan, Victor Borge, George Gobel and Edgar Bergen, all at the beginning of their careers, were entertaining members.

Prohibition required legal establishments to play by the rules. At the DAC, that meant no drinks in public areas. According to Hughes, captains and waiters were fired by the score for infractions. Hughes charged that speakeasies were getting dozens of club members every night, while "clubs and hotels have taken it on the chin during Prohibition, one of the most absurdly unfair business chronicles in history." By the time Prohibition ended in April 1933, the ban had taken a heavy toll—a loss in gross DAC revenue of $2.5 million over fifteen years.

But alcohol sales alone could not overcome the G-force of the Depression. Resident entry fees were lowered from $500 to $300 and briefly to $100 in a bid to attract members. Dues were cut drastically to $5 a month for residents for six months, and then $7.50 a month. Lower rates had the desired effect: new members. A banker, 1934 president William Lerchen, nudged the entrance fees up to $200 in April.

As the year drew to a close, things were looking up; November brought in $5,600 profit. December was also healthy, with $120,000 in sales generated by holiday parties such as those hosted by the Chrysler Corporation and the *New York Times*. By year's end, the DAC had 2,729 resident members.

The DAC recovered much more quickly than other places. The New Year's Eve party to usher in 1935 was successful, and that January was the most profitable first month of the year in club history. That year, the club celebrated its twentieth anniversary in high style. Three orchestras played, a grand supper was served and members were awed by a colossal 1,348-pound anniversary cake.

As 1935 began, the DAC was led by the man who would shape Chrysler Corporation into the world's second-largest automotive producer, K.T. Keller. On the national scene, FDR created the Works Progress Administration, which resulted in thousands of jobs for Detroiters. Detroit earned the title "City of Champions" in 1935, with the Red Wings winning the Stanley Cup, the Tigers clinching the World Series and the Lions taking the national football championship. Even the DAC's outdoor swim team captured the national championship in 1935; its premier diver, Dick Degener, would take a gold medal in the 1936 Olympics. Added to this mix were club member and champion speedboat racer Gar Wood, still thrilling crowds along the Detroit riverfront with his powerful series of Miss America crafts, and soon-to-be world champion boxer Joe Louis. Detroit was on the way up, and so was the club.

Keller's administration was just one sweet song, with the club making a reasonable amount of money from operations and carrying to surplus a total of $35,357. The number of new members elected and former members reinstated reached 166 by early 1936. That allowed for some needed improvements—a redesign of the busy bowling center and the creation of the Tap Room, at $20,000 apiece.

In April, club employees earned raises of 6 percent. In the summer of 1936, the DAC was promoting the club's modern new air conditioning system, a $40,000 investment. The ease with which the club adapted to new trends was important in its ability to remain vital. At the end of his term, Keller left the club in the finest financial shape in history.

Another of the automotive pioneering Fisher brothers, Edward Fisher, became DAC president in 1936. In June, the Tap Room was dedicated, featuring Dean Cornwell's *Treaty of Lancaster* mural. In October, a new ladies' cocktail lounge debuted.

Although the worst was over for the club, the last few years of the 1930s had ups and downs, including a 1937 workers' strike that resulted in wages being restored to 1929 levels.

President of the largest Midwest dealer of machinery, Charles Bush led the DAC in 1938. While the club lost $7,564 in operations, it remained solid, with over $400,000 in cash and securities on hand. Under the leadership of General Motors president William Knudsen, the club ended with an $185,000 surplus.

The DAC had weathered a difficult decade and emerged strong. In 1940, the club marked its twenty-fifth anniversary with weeklong celebrations. The Depression became a fading memory.

Chapter 15

MODERN DAC ATHLETIC HEROES

As the new club grew, so, too, did its bowling, squash, handball, swimming, diving and boxing programs, producing new athletes, many of whose achievements remain within the clubhouse walls. New clubs within the club sprang up—the Beavers, the Blackballers and the Bowlers—offering team and individual competition. The hiring of coaches, trainers and athletic directors by the club—people like Matt Mann, Fred Hammond, Victor E. Tomlinson, Norman Ross, the legendary Clarence Pinkston and Rex Aubrey—helped keep the DAC active in amateur sports. Mainly, the club remained closely connected to amateur sports, producing more than a dozen Olympians. To date, thirty-three DAC members—professional and amateur athletes, coaches, team owners and sportswriters—have been inducted into the Michigan Sports Hall of Fame.

At only five feet, two inches tall and by his own admission not much of an athlete, Henry Jamison "Jam" Handy created waves of awe among swimmers with his unusual technique and set world records through innovation that revolutionized the sport. The Olympic medal winner is credited with inventing the modern, head-down breathing technique for the Australian Crawl, the "legless crawl," the painting of lines on the bottom of a pool so swimmers could see where they were going, being the first to use the alternative arm stroke in the backstroke and narrowing the kick of the breaststroke. He won national championships in the breaststroke, backstroke and crawl. Handy won an Olympic bronze in 1904 in the 440-yard breaststroke. After the Olympics, he set a number of world records, including the 880-yard and 1,500-yard freestyle in 1906, the 100-yard backstroke and 220-yard breaststroke in 1907 and the 150-yard backstroke in 1909.

In 1907, he was diagnosed with an enlarged heart. Doctors explained that he needed to use the extra capacity or his heart would rupture. So Handy added water polo to his repertoire. Water polo would lead him to another Olympic appearance as a member of the U.S. water polo team in 1924 (two years before he joined the DAC), but the team did not medal. He turned to marathon competitions, winning the national AAU's ten-mile Mississippi River Swim Marathon three times. Handy formed the Jam Handy Organization in 1911, credited with developing slide film projectors and the 170-degree wide-angle lens and producing seven thousand films for the army during World War II.

The DAC's aquatic director and coach, Matt Mann, had no doubt that Tedford Cann, a star swimmer at the club and a national champion, would make the 1920 U.S. Olympic team. He knew that no one could beat Cann in the 100-yard freestyle. Cann became the first man in the history of American aquatics to win every freestyle event in a single competition, all at the 1920 AAU nationals. He also became the first in the world that year to break 2:20 for a 220-yard race.

But then fate dealt its blow when Cann was involved in an automobile accident that took the life of another swimming star, Arthur McAleenan. Cann's leg was so badly fractured that he was unable to compete in the games, and it was predicted that he would never swim with the same proficiency again.

His swimming ability may have won him world records and would have undoubtedly earned him gold at the Olympics, but in 1917, it also saved his life and all those onboard the navy ship USS *May*. The young navy seaman was onboard when the vessel sprung a leak between Bermuda and the Azores. For over an hour, he faced the freezing Atlantic as he dove inside and outside his ship to block the leak. When the feat was completed, Cann was exhausted, but the ship made it safely to the Azores. His act of heroism earned him a Medal of Honor, the first given by the United States during the First World War.

Clarence and Betty Pinkston hold a special place in DAC history. The couple made their way to Detroit in 1927, when Clarence, known as "Pink," became the swimming instructor and later athletic director at the

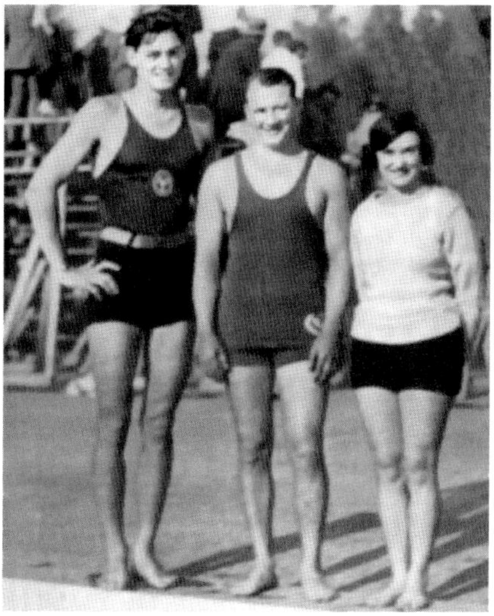

Clarence and Betty Pinkston with Johnny Weissmuller. DAC News *archives*.

club during a career that spanned thirty-five years. The two Olympic divers were fun-loving and dedicated athletes and coaches to the sports they loved and shared.

The Pinkstons, who between them have seven Olympic diving medals, both started out in other sports. Betty, born Elizabeth Anne Becker, began as a swimmer after a case of diphtheria at eight left her with a nervous condition. She began frequenting a Turngemeinde, a type of athletic club popular during the early 1900s, and by twelve was swimming competitively, but it was not her sport of choice.

Betty turned her interest to diving, and by fifteen, her career was underway. She won the Middle Atlantic Association AAU title and moved from her native Philadelphia to Atlantic City to practice at a better pool. She also won national championships for one-meter, three-meter and springboard.

Pinkston, on the other hand, began as a gymnast. Raised in San Diego, he also frequented a Turngemeinde. He was determined to become an athlete, and at fifteen, he became a Pacific Coast Champion in gymnastics. Pinkston didn't start diving until he attended Stanford. There, he realized his gymnastic skills would not win him the gold, but he had a strong desire to go to the Olympics. He began applying his skills to diving and discovered he had talent. He won the first event he appeared in and never lost one until the 1920 Olympic games. He won seven AAU championships—five for platform diving and two for springboard diving. He invented a new dive, the full twisting one and a half.

At the 1920 Olympics in Antwerp, Pinkston won the gold medal for platform diving and the silver for springboard. Those games, however, were a sore point for Betty, who tried out for the Olympic team and tied for third place but wasn't chosen to go.

After winning the nationals in 1924, she went to California for the Olympic trials, where she met Pinkston. They made the team together and later traveled to the Olympics in Paris, where they began their courtship. Their love proved good luck. Betty won the gold for springboard and the silver for platform, and Pinkston won the bronze for springboard and platform.

While in Europe, the two tried to marry with Olympic medal winner Johnny Weissmuller, of later Tarzan fame, as their best man, but when the plan failed, they both headed back to the States, Pinkston to San Diego and Betty to Philadelphia. They married later in the year with Olympic diving coach Fred Cady as their best man.

In 1926, Betty won the three-meter at the national AAU championships, and the Pinkstons relocated to Detroit. At the DAC pool, Betty continued to train for the 1928 Olympics, with Pink as her coach. She won her second gold for platform diving.

In 1936, Pinkston coached Elbert Root and Dick Degener at the Berlin Olympics. Pink attended the games, where Degener won a gold medal and Root a silver, but his official role as a diving coach with the U.S. men's team is unclear.

He was selective about those he coached. Jeanne (Stunyo) Korpack, an Olympic diver who trained under Pink in the mid-1950s, remembers that he had so much experience that he would look at someone and know whether they "had it" or not. At the club, Pink had his "swimming dolls" and was instrumental in making the DAC Beavers what they are today.

Betty was also an involved coach. She turned pro and started teaching swimming at the Detroit Golf Club. She was the first one to teach 1952 gold medal winner Clark Scholes, whom Pink later also coached, how to swim.

In 1966, Pink was inducted into the International Swimming Hall of Fame as an outstanding coach. Pink, who died in 1961 at age sixty-one, is also a member of the Helms Hall of Fame and the San Diego Hall of Fame. Betty was inducted into the International Swimming Hall of Fame in 1967.

Dipping himself into the dyed runoff of the sluiceways from Leeds, England's wool mills, Matt Mann would return home blue, brown, red or whatever color the mills were dyeing wool that day. On one occasion, he went skinny-dipping in a canal and his clothes were stolen. A police officer marched him through town, naked, to the police station. Nothing would stop Mann from swimming when the compulsion overcame him, not even work.

When he couldn't swim, Mann would coach, becoming the most prolific swimming coach in the nation with the University of Michigan, the University of Oklahoma and, briefly in the 1920s, the DAC.

Mann learned to swim at age eight in the Leeds public baths. The baths were changed twice a week, and it only cost a penny to swim on "dirty-water" days, so Mann would scrape up a penny for a dip. By the time he was nine, Mann was England's boy champion. When he was fourteen, he won England's senior championship.

He is the only person to coach swimming at both Harvard and Yale and also coached for the New York Athletic Club. In December 1918, Mann commandeered the DAC swim team and led it to an upset victory over the YMCA only days after being hired by the DAC. It was the first time the DAC had ever beaten the Y, which fielded formidable teams in those days. Mann trained such swimming stalwarts as Tedford Cann, Norman Ross and Margaret Woodbridge Presley in the DAC's pool. Ross and Presley won four gold medals and a silver between them at the 1920 Olympics.

Mann was so completely enveloped in the world of swimming that, at the same time he was coaching at the DAC, he also coached the New York Athletic Club, Yale, Brooklyn's Poly Prep and Navy all in the same season.

In 1923, with the Olympics approaching, Mann agreed to help the University of Michigan swim program. He put together a remarkable string of championships at U of M. The Wolverines completely dominated the Big Ten from 1927 until 1948, during which time they won sixteen team championships. They also took four straight NCAA team championships from 1937 to 1941.

In 1952, Mann was named coach of the U.S. men's Olympic swimming team in Helsinki. Mann's swimmers won six gold, three silver and two bronze medals.

In the 1930s, while the Detroit Athletic Club's swimmers were leaving opponents in their wake, Dick Degener was making "little splash" as a diver. And he received plenty of attention for it. Degener was the winner of two Olympic medals and fourteen national championships.

"Dick Degener…made springboard diving something of a new art form in the 30's and…was fondly described as the 'Fred Astaire of diving,'" wrote George E. Van in the *Detroit News*.

Degener went undefeated swimming at U of M, winning three Big Ten titles and three NCAA titles. He also made a trip to the Los Angeles Olympics in 1932 but missed the two-and-a-half somersault he had performed to perfection the previous year. The error cost Degener a gold medal, but he earned a bronze.

Degener left U of M in 1934 with an Olympic medal, three Big Ten titles and three NCAA titles. He then came to the DAC to train under Pinkston. Almost immediately, he brought a championship to the DAC, winning the

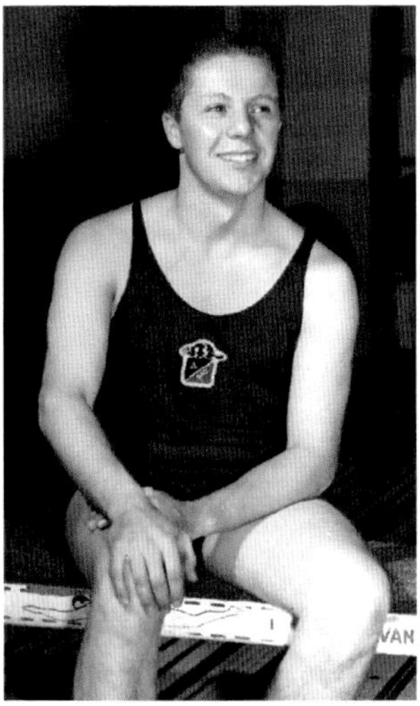

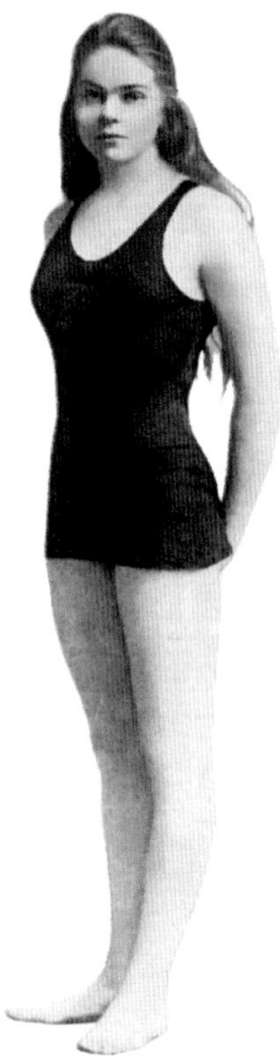

AAU national outdoor meet at the Chicago World's Fair.

Degener earned a trip to the 1936 Olympics in Munich. In the competition, he was in second place, behind teammate Marshall Wayne, in the springboard competition with one dive remaining. Degener performed an almost-perfect one-and-a-half somersault while Wayne faltered on his dive, and Degener won the gold medal.

The year 1920 marked the appearance of the first U.S. Olympic women's swimming team. On this history-making team was eighteen-year-old Margaret Woodbridge Presley, among the first great female athletes to train at the DAC. Under the expert training of Mann, Presley won a gold medal in the Antwerp games that year as a member of the women's four-hundred-meter relay squad and a silver medal for the three-hundred-meter freestyle swim, which she won in world-record time.

When Presley first began gaining attention in 1919, she'd only been swimming for one year. She graduated in the mid-1920s from the City College of Detroit, predecessor to Wayne State University. She was a swimming letter winner and was the third woman to be inducted into the Wayne State University Athletic Hall of Fame.

Ray Konopatsky had little future as a swimmer at Cass Technical High School. He tried out for the team but didn't make it, so he began swimming at the St. Clair Recreation Center under the tutelage of Frank Butler and

Top: Dick Degener, fourteen-time national champion and Olympic gold medal winner. *DAC archives.*

Bottom: Margaret Woodbridge Presley. *DAC archives.*

impressed the Detroit Athletic Club's Clarence Pinkston. Konopatsky was tall (well over six feet) and lean—a perfect specimen for Pinkston to mold into a champion. The DAC knows Konopatsky as Ray Kaye, former Beaver president, Olympian and national breaststroke champion.

Like many of Pinkston's protégés, Kaye would become a national champion. In 1935, Kaye set records in the two-hundred-meter and five-hundred-meter breaststroke. He was the AAU national champion in the breastroke for 1936 and made the U.S. Olympic swim team. At those same championships, Kaye and two other DAC swimmers, Taylor Drysdale and Jim Gilhula, set a world record in the three-hundred-meter medley relay. At the Olympics, Kaye finished seventh in his breastroke event. He went on to win another national championship in the two-hundred-meter breaststroke in 1937.

In the late 1930s, Halina Tomska Papp was heralded as one of the best female swimmers ever developed in Michigan. The Detroit native was trained at the DAC under Pinkston. During her swimming career, she broke down many barriers. She was the first woman to beat one minute in the 100-yard freestyle; she won four National AAU championships and set national records in 150- and 200-meter and 220- and 440-yard freestyle events; and she was a relay swimmer who helped set three American relay records and one world relay record.

At one time, Papp and her brother Waldemar Tomska were considered the fastest female and male swimmers in the world. Papp, who narrowly missed a chance at the 1936 Olympics, made the 1940 Olympic team set for Tokyo, but with World War II, the games were cancelled.

Pinkston trained his share of swimming champions, but he had a couple of champion divers, including Elbert Root, who came to the DAC from Florida to train with Pinkston. He specialized in the low platform and ten-meter platform and won a national championship on the low board in 1935 and later Olympic silver during the 1936 Berlin games.

Taylor Drysdale was not only an excellent swimmer but got to work under two of best coaches in the business: Pinskton at the DAC and Matt Mann at U of M. Drysdale was an exceptional backstroker, dominating the college circuit. At the University of Michigan, he never lost an intercollegiate race in any stroke, including dual meets, during his three years of competition (1932–35), according to his biography for induction in the International Swimming Hall of Fame. Drysdale won three NCAA championships in those years. In the non-Olympic 300 IM, he broke Buster Crabbe's American record and held it for two years. He also competed in three international competitions, and during the war years of 1941–46, he was the European Theater backstroke and IM champion.

Drysdale helped set an American record in 1936 at the National AAU swimming championships in Des Moines, swimming the backstroke leg of the three-hundred-meter medley relay with DAC stars Ray Kaye and James Gilhula. At the 1936 Berlin Olympics, he finished fourth in the one-hundred-meter backstroke, one second away from a bronze medal.

James Gilhula has a permanent place in the pantheon of DAC athletics as an Olympian and national champion. Gilhula came to the DAC in 1928 from California. He graduated from Detroit's Southeastern High School, and like so many other swimmers, he blossomed under the tutelage of Pinkston.

Gilhula set a state record in the 500-meter freestyle, swimming it in 6:00.6. That record was eventually broken by another DAC swimmer, Tom Haynie, who knocked 15 seconds off Gilhula's mark. Gilhula was also a national champion in 1931 in both the 100-yard and 220-yard freestyle events.

The early days of DAC bowling found several athletes worthy of recognition. Fred S. Smith stands among the best. Considered one of the best left-handed bowlers in the country, he was the first club bowling champion in 1916 and, in 1925, became the first member to bowl a perfect 300 on the DAC lanes. In 1936, he toured continental Europe with nine American bowlers, staging competitions and exhibitions in conjunction with the Olympics in Berlin.

Smith was already a highly regarded bowler on the local and national levels when he came to the DAC in 1916. He enrolled on account of his father, Herman Schmidt, who was also among the top bowlers at the club. Over the next twenty-five years, Smith (who had Anglicized his name from Schmidt) remained popular at the DAC. He won the club championship six times and was all-events winner three times in the Inter-Club event.

At the pinnacle of his achievements, during a tough competition, Smith bowled his 300 game.

In many ways, he remains first among a long line of DAC bowlers, a history that includes Dawson Taylor, Fred Wolf and Joe Paulus.

Of the twenty-six American wrestlers who competed in the 1920 Olympics, only Charles Edwin Ackerly, later a DAC member, came back with a gold medal, which he won in the featherweight division. Ackerly was captain of the Cornell University wrestling team.

On the first day of the Olympic trials in 1956, DAC diver Jeanne (Stunyo) Korpak was in first place for springboard diving. The second day, everything changed. With each consecutive dive she watched her rank drop lower on the large scoreboard over the pool until she was placed fourth.

In an interview, Korpak once said, "I had one dive left, and it happened to be my favorite and the one I had the most confidence in." By the time she'd finished, she knew it was perfect. The dive received the highest score during the event.

But her Olympic chances were still slim. Ranked third in springboard was Paula Jean Myers. Myers had already made the team for tower diving. Korpak knew Myers was diving right after her and performing the same dive. She was hiding when Myers performed the fated dive that lowered her score, thus elevating Korpak to third place.

Korpak remembered that all the Detroit photographers and the Pinkstons were looking for her while she was behind a curtain crying. She came out to paparazzi-style flashes. Everyone wanted a picture of the "Detroit Twins," as Korpak and her diving partner, Barbara Gilders Dudeck, were often nicknamed.

As a young girl, Korpak rode forty minutes by train by herself to Chicago three times a week for practice. Her swimming coach didn't know anything about diving but knew enough to know that she had talent. He also knew one of the top coaches in the country, Clarence Pinkston. During a meet in Detroit in 1951, he asked Pinkston to watch her dive. Pinkston helped arrange for Korpak to live with a local family. Korpak, fifteen at the time, moved from her hometown to begin training in Detroit.

Along with Dudeck, she trained at the club under Pinkston in the 1950s. Korpak won the silver for springboard at the 1956 Olympics in Melbourne, placed second at nationals five times and was second in the Pan-American Games in 1955.

Dudeck remembers her first visit to the Detroit Athletic Club in 1953. The teenage diver was auditioning for Clarence Pinkston after a mutual acquaintance, gold medalist and diver Bob Clotworthy, arranged a meeting. Seeing talent and potential in the young athlete, Pinkston asked her to come back.

Later, Pinkston confided in Dudeck that he'd taken her on because another diver he was training, Korpak, was by herself and he thought they'd be good competition for each other. While the competition between the two did encourage both to try harder, Dudeck proved herself an exceptional athlete in her own right. Under Pinkston, she won three United States Championships, placed fourth for springboard diving at the 1956 Olympics and took third in the 1959 Pan-American games.

The judges conferred by the pool, looking at their watches with doubt. *Was it possible anyone could swim that fast?* they wondered.

The great Johnny Weissmuller—the unbeatable Johnny Weissmuller—held the record for the one-hundred-yard freestyle, swimming it in fifty-one seconds flat. But at the national championship meet at Yale in 1942, William Prew would swim so fast people couldn't believe it—actually refused to believe it.

Earlier that year, Prew had won the NCAA championship, but he was looking forward to competing against the best in the nation at the Amateur Athletic Union championship. In the AAU semifinals, Prew swam the one-hundred-yard event in 51.2 seconds, only a hair's width away from the record.

Prew, the club's 1970 president, was one of Clarence Pinkston's many protégés. He became an all-American at Wayne University in the one-hundred-yard freestyle and on two medley relay teams. On one of those relays, he swam with another outstanding DAC swimmer, Taylor Drysdale. Prew was also the NCAA one-hundred-yard freestyle champion in 1942 before his record-breaking race at Yale.

By all accounts, Prew was a sure bet to win an Olympic gold medal in 1940, but the competition was cancelled. He was inducted into the International Swimming Hall of Fame as a pioneer member in 1998.

Second-generation DAC member Clarke Scholes lifted his head from the water and looked to his left. Goran Larrson was somewhere behind him. When Scholes turned to his right, he was staring straight into the eyes of Hiroshi Suzuki, three lanes away. They wondered the same thing: who had won?

It was the first medal event of the 1952 Olympics in Helsinki—the men's one-hundred-meter freestyle—and Scholes and Suzuki were awaiting official word on who had won the gold medal. By stopwatch, both swimmers would finish with the same time—57.4 seconds. A dead heat. "But when the Japanese came over and congratulated me, I knew I had won," Scholes finished. By sight, Scholes touched the wall less than half a stroke ahead of Suzuki.

Scholes had won both the 1950 NCAA championship and the AAU national championship in the one-hundred-yard freestyle. In 1951, Scholes won the Big

Ten and NCAA championships in the fifty-yard and one-hundred-yard freestyle and swam a leg on the championship 4x100 relay team. In 1952, he captained the Michigan State swim team and hit a grand slam in the one-hundred-yard freestyle. He won the Big Ten championship and the NCAA championship, being named an all-American for the third consecutive year. He also won the AAU championship and the crown jewel, the Olympic gold medal.

Longtime DAC member Bernard Pat Costello began rowing in 1948, when a friend invited him to the Detroit Boat Club. It took until his freshman year in college for Costello to find his niche. In rowing, which he said he got into "by accident," he excelled, attending the 1952 Olympics and winning silver at the 1956 Olympics.

The United States took the silver medal in the four-oared shell rowing category without a coxswain in the 1956 games. On the team was Detroit native Jim McIntosh. At the time, McIntosh was a member of the DAC trained at the Detroit Boat Club.

The only boxer to win four NCAA titles (while at Michigan State), famed DAC member Chuck Davey, also competed in the 1948 Olympics and went on to a professional career, winning forty-two bouts against formidable opponents including Rocky Graziano and Carmen Basilio.

Davey later served as boxing commissioner for the state of Michigan. The DAC Chuck Davey Boxing Classic tournament, featuring boxers from the U.S. military academies, is held each year in his honor. Davey died in 2002 due to complications from a swimming accident that left him paralyzed.

At the annual DAC Golf Outing one year, Joe Paulus was greeted with a standing ovation from 144 of his fellow members. The man known as "The Legend" around the club was being congratulated for turning eighty-four.

Paulus's nickname is no surprise. Over four decades (beginning in the 1960s), he won fifteen Club Individual Championships for bowling and was runner-up thirteen times. In addition, he claimed his first team club bowling championship in 2001. That win capped a long list of accomplishments—twenty-six Club titles, forty consecutive Interclub events and the DAC's first eight hundred series.

Paulus's story begins in 1929 at the age of twelve, when his father, John Paulus, built Chene-Trombly Recreation, one of the first bowling establishments in Detroit. Joe was a member and the president for seven years of the Detroit Times All-Star Traveling Classic. At twenty-seven, he became

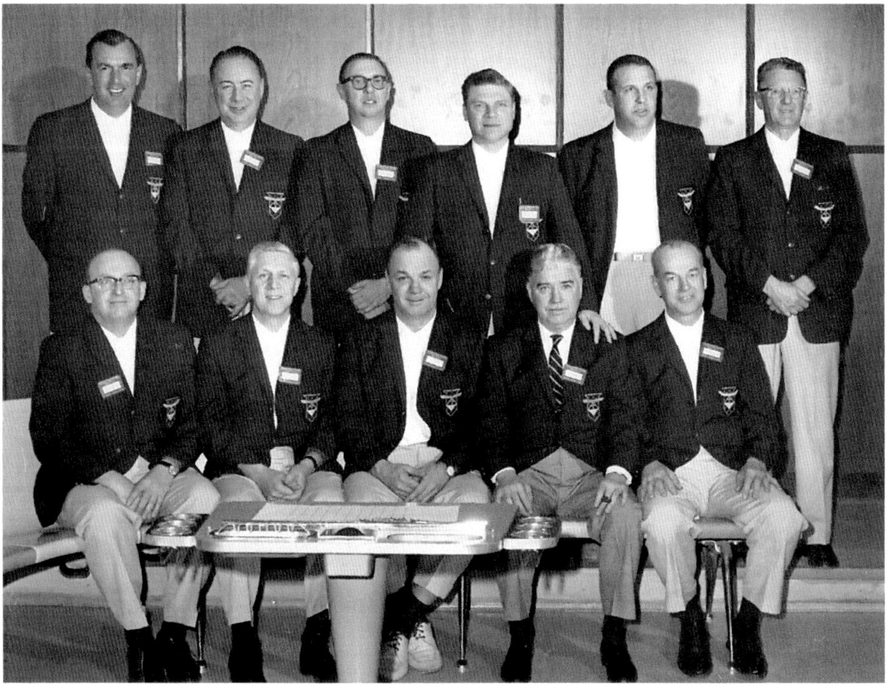

Joe Paulus (seated second from left) with other great DAC bowlers. *DAC archives.*

the youngest president of the Bowling Proprietors Association of Greater Detroit. At forty-one, he became the youngest president of the Bowling Proprietors Association of America. He also served as vice-president and then president of the National Bowling Council.

On March 31, 1979, he rolled the first ever 800 series at the DAC with games of 290, 258 and 257. Six years later, on March 25, 1985, he garnered his first 300 game at the club. Paulus has been named Bowler of the Century by the DAC and captain of the honorary DAC All-Century Bowling Team. In recognition of his skill, the club began the Paulus Cup for outstanding senior bowlers.

Two of Detroit's great professional sports teams were born at the Detroit Athletic Club. Both the Lions and the Red Wings owe their existence to the efforts of members of the DAC. In addition, eight of the ten owners of the Detroit Tigers over 111 years have been DAC members.

Longtime club secretary Charlie Hughes was instrumental in the 1926 formation of the Detroit Hockey Club, later to become the Red Wings.

Hughes's personal efforts led DAC members interested in a new sport for the city to create the Detroit Hockey Club (he soon became its president). He raised the $100,000 needed to purchase the entire reserve list of the Victoria Cougars of the Western Hockey League.

The team, known as the Detroit Cougars, suffered through a shaky first season. During that lackluster first year, the Cougars played in Windsor while Hughes organized the construction of a sporting arena named Olympia. In 1927, the team moved into Olympia, built by Hughes and his syndicate, and retained Jack Adams as coach, beginning his thirty-five-year association with the team. The team got a new look in the early 1930s and became the Detroit Falcons for a time before James Norris bought the team and renamed it the Detroit Red Wings.

In 1934, in the depths of the Depression, DAC member G.A. Richards took an audacious leap of faith, buying a bankrupt Ohio pro football team, the Portsmith Spartans. He moved the franchise to Detroit and renamed them the Lions. His "leap" in 1934 was daring not only because of the Depression but also because three pro football teams had already failed in Detroit. Nineteen DAC members joined Richards in the venture, and together they put up $23,000 to buy the franchise and its debts. Richards, owner of the radio station WJR, and his partners took over the team in April 1934 and promptly renamed the Lions.

After three weeks of practice, the Lions opened the 1934 season and went on to win the first ten games they played. They also established the Thanksgiving Day game. The next few seasons were lackluster, and in 1941, Richards sold the team to Chicago department store executive Fred Mandel. Mandel later sold the team back to Detroit interests headed by DAC member D.F. Fife. The 1950s were the Lions' heyday, and by 1961, DAC member William Clay Ford was elected president of the team. Four years later, he bought out all the Lions stockholders to become sole owner.

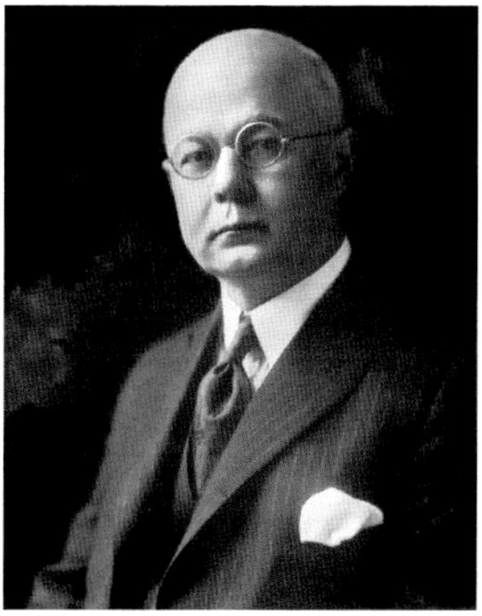

Frank Navin, Detroit Tigers owner and DAC president. *DAC archives.*

As for the Tigers, the long association with the DAC began with first owner James Burns in 1901 and continues to the present day with Mike Illitch, who bought the team in 1992.

You can't have a discussion about athletics at the DAC without mentioning the three Bs—the Beavers, Blackballers and Bowlers.

There have always been swimming Beavers at the DAC even before the group was formalized in 1919. Bowling as a member sport dates to the original club on Woodward before taking on a life of its own once the doors to the new club opened in 1915. The Blackballers, too, have been around in one fashion or another since the first handball and squash courts opened up in 1915.

By all accounts, handball was the most popular game in the early years, while interest in squash racquets waned, especially during World War I. Leading the handball charge was the DAC's first athletic director, Vic Tomlinson, who teamed with club champion A.L.C. Henry to win the U.S. Doubles Championship in 1917. The following year, the club hosted the National Handball Championships, focusing attention on the DAC as home to top-notch handball. By 1922, some ninety-six members had entered the club's handball championships.

At the same time, bowling began its climb to the top of the sports heap. In 1915, there were six wood lanes with a few benches for players and spectators. The first season included a Thursday night league with six five-man teams. The league played thirty games, or ten series, and a trophy was offered to the winning team. The winning team was captained by E.B. Forbes, a member of the first bowling committee, a group chaired by W.J. Chittenden Jr.

Not long after the season ended, an invitation was received from the Columbus Athletic Club to join it in an after-season "interclub" tournament along with the Cleveland Athletic Club and the Pittsburgh Athletic Association. Each club would field its top six bowlers. The invite was accepted, and the DAC finished a "bad fourth." Undaunted, Forbes invited the other clubs to Detroit a year later.

The DAC entered a team in the 1916 ocean-to-ocean telegraphic match, in which a dozen athletic clubs competed. The games were bowled by each club on its own lanes, and scores were transmitted by wire as each frame was bowled. The DAC finished second with 2,895, bested only by the Seattle Athletic Club.

Interest in bowling waned during the First World War, and it wasn't until 1920 that the DAC could field a team to win the annual Interclub Tournament. That year, the club championship was awarded to Forbes, who managed a 191 average.

Meanwhile, down at poolside, a group of DAC swimming enthusiasts was gathering on a brisk day in January 1919 to form the Beavers. This first club within the club was organized to meet for lunch each week at poolside and host a monthly handicapped swim meet. And so the Beavers were born—the brainchild of E.A. Laitner, Harold Butcher, A.H. Williamson, Ed Henkel and A. Ward Copley. Its members numbered a mere twenty. Within two months, though, they had grown to more than one hundred.

Famed swim coach Matt Mann would coach the Beavers and lead his teams in state and national championship competitions.

By 1921, the group was requiring members to swim twenty-five yards before they could wear the Beaver mantle. That year also saw the first "barrage" of rolls launched by Beavers at a guest speaker.

The Beavers quickly gained a national reputation for producing champion swimmers and by the mid-1920s had grown to three hundred—the largest swim club in the world. A new coach, Norman Ross, arrived and soon presided over the first Beaver game called "pullaway," a variation of tag played in and under water. In 1926, the game changed to water baseball, but then Ross left and the club hired Clarence Pinkston as athletic director in 1927.

Two years earlier, the club had added two roof courts for the squash players, and some sixty players entered the annual handicap tournament.

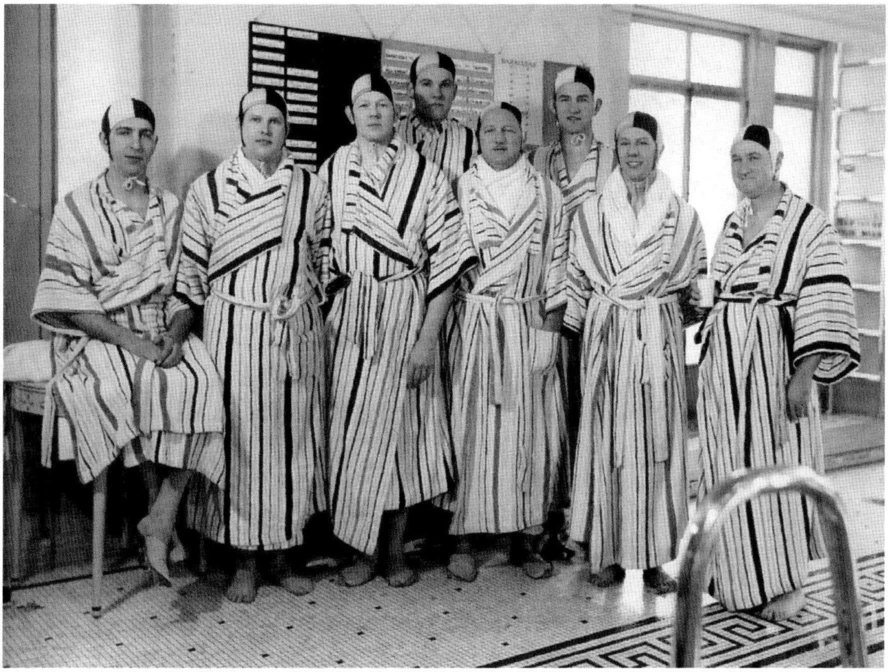

The Beavers on deck in striped robes. *DAC archives.*

The national championships were hosted by the DAC that year, and interclub teams were entered in Detroit's leagues.

With squash growing in popularity, the club converted a handball court for doubles squash, and by, 1929 another handball court had gone over to squash. Dominant players included E.J. Smith, who won four handball singles, three handball doubles and two squash singles titles; and T.N. Bourke, who won nine squash championships (1923–31). By 1937, the handball players had formed the Handball Club. Three years later, the group expanded to include squash players and became known as the Squash-Handball Association.

Down in the bowling center, the keglers were also growing. In 1925 and 1927, the DAC initiated home tournaments with the Buffalo and Cleveland clubs, in addition to the regular Interclub matches. The Depression stifled the DAC bowling program at first, but by 1935–36, the number of bowlers and leagues had quadrupled. Two new lanes were also added. About 1940, Buffalo replaced Columbus as the fourth club in the annual Interclub Tournament.

Up on the fourth floor, a new game was entering the club's lexicon: "basketbrawl." Even then the rules for the game were few, but the play was rough (and still is), and Beavers loved it. As the club struggled through the Depression, the Beavers roster continued to grow (there were, and remain, both "land" and "swimming" Beavers).

The annual Old Club Outing began in 1937. The highlight of the day was the Beavers-Bowlers baseball game. The first match was won by the Beavers. The 1940 season ushered in the current individual point scoring system, and though the swim races have changed a bit, the University of Detroit Presidents Trophy still awaits the top swimmer of the year.

That decade also saw the start of the "mega speaker," and for twenty years the Beavers featured names like Jack Dempsey, Ed Sullivan, Ann Landers and Jesse Owens. Since then, many noted sports and entertainment celebrities have graced the Beavers stage.

Meanwhile, the Squash-Handball Association continued to see a string of great champions, including Norm Fredericks Sr., who won sixteen singles and eleven doubles handball titles (1942–69); Bob Den Uyl, who claimed eleven singles and nineteen doubles handball titles (1958–85); John Reindel, who won fifteen squash titles (1936–58); and, more recently, George Haggarty, who won twenty titles (1968–90).

By 1947, there was a boom in squash and handball, and for the first time in DAC history, there were more than one hundred squash players. In 1962, squash courts on the fourth floor were remodeled. Hashim Kahn, probably the greatest squash player of all time, played an exhibition match with Eddie Hahn to dedicate the refinished courts.

By the 1960s, the Blackballers had grown to two hundred members. It was then that the group took off under the guidance of the new athletic director, a young Aussie named Rex Aubrey.

The longevity and popularity of bowling continued. In 1955, the first meeting of the Twenty-Five-Year Club was held. Today there are more than 150 members of that group. Automatic pin setters were installed in 1957 and new lanes in 1963, along with high-speed ball returns. The year 1966–67 saw the beginning of the DAC Club Team Championships; the Monday 8:30 league won the honors. The following year saw the first DAC Doubles Tournament, won by Don Dykstra and Lee Schoenith.

At poolside, the Beavers' reputation as pranksters continued to grow, as did the group's litany of speakers (including Howard Cosell, Bo Schembechler, Jack Nicklaus, Ted Turner and Arnold Palmer). The year 1962 featured the start of Rex Aubrey's reign as athletic director. The Beavers, which peaked at 1,200 members during the 1970s, today claim nearly 1,000 members.

As the Beavers grew, so did the Blackballers. By 1990, the DAC had dramatically expanded its court facilities, adding three handball and three squash courts. From fifty players in 1937, there are now nearly six hundred Blackballers competing in squash, racquetball, handball and basketball.

By the 1970s, the DAC could claim (and still does) the largest bowling program in the country. To show its muscle, the DAC fielded forty teams at the ABC Tournament in Detroit's Cobo Hall in 1971, and some eight hundred people attended the group's ladies' party that year.

In the early 1980s, the original Interclub Tournament ended when Pittsburgh withdrew. The tournament was revamped in 1982–83 and continues today. There are nearly nine hundred bowlers at the DAC, taking to the lanes in over twenty-two leagues.

Chapter 16

THE "GHQ" OF THE ARSENAL OF DEMOCRACY

By 1940, the Depression was over, Prohibition was history and the wheels of progress were turning in the factories and boardrooms of Detroit. The new decade ushered in the era of big bands, big cars and a steady drumbeat toward war that already engulfed Europe and parts of Asia.

As the meeting place for the city's industrial elite, the DAC played a key role in World War II as "general headquarters" for the "Arsenal of Democracy," the place where auto magnates laid plans to steer production of an endless stream of bombers, tanks, jeeps, trucks, guns and other munitions. Detroit, the automotive capital of the world, in very short order redirected its massive output from cars to military goods essential for victory.

Overseeing this Herculean task with speed and efficiency was a captain of industry handpicked for the job by President Roosevelt: William S. Knudsen, the leader of General Motors Corporation and the club's 1939 president. The humble Danish immigrant who worked his way up from a machinist to oversee the largest automaker in the world was put in charge of the War Production Board in June 1940. Four months later, Knudsen summoned directors of the Automobile Manufacturing Association to the DAC to enlist support in taking on defense contracts.

Club members Edsel Ford, C.W. Nash, Alvan Macauley, C.E. Wilson, Alfred Sloan, George Mason, S.E. Skinner and I.B. Babcock were among twenty-two leaders seated around the table to create the Automotive Council for Air Defense. With a mastery of mass production, a wide network of suppliers and a huge workforce of skilled laborers, the automakers were well poised for the job.

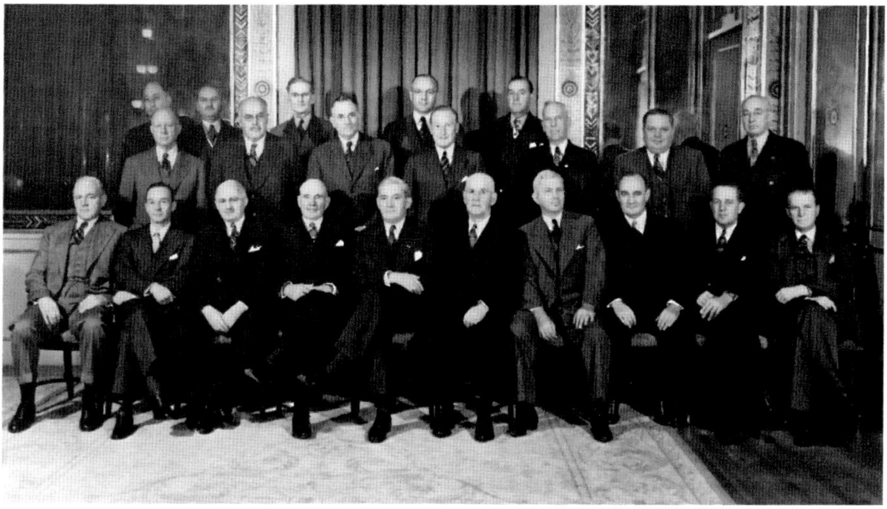

William Knudsen (seated fifth from left) and fellow automakers committed to defense manufacturing at the DAC in 1940. *DAC archives.*

To appreciate the magnitude of what Knudsen was asking his competitors, consider that they were selling more cars in 1940 than any year since before the Depression. Yet to a man, they agreed to take on defense production.

Knudsen turned to K.T. Keller, president of Chrysler Corporation, to build a new plant to produce thirty-ton medium tanks. By the spring of 1941, tanks were coming off the line at a factory in Warren, eventually twenty-five thousand in total.

No American city carried out more defense work than metro Detroit. Of the $200 billion awarded in contracts, $50 billion went to automakers. Designers worked around the clock to create complicated products with thousands of parts. By the time of Pearl Harbor, American production had surpassed what had taken Germany five years to accomplish.

As the nation ramped up for war, the club was enjoying its best financial position ever. By the spring of 1941, there were 2,800 resident members and a small army on the waiting list. The club increased its liquor stock to prepare for wartime shortages, buying $250,000 of fine wines and spirits.

With war officially declared in December, the DAC went into support mode, sending cigarettes, magazines and playing cards to Michigan soldiers in four army camps. In January 1942, Knudsen was relieved of his job. Roosevelt commissioned him a U.S. Army lieutenant general, and he spent the war years checking on weapons production cross country and abroad.

In order to meet the voracious demand for military goods, the War Production Board halted car and light truck production on January 30, 1942. For the first time in forty years, Detroit was out of the auto business, instead racing to fill military contracts.

A new atmosphere settled into the clubhouse. DAC weddings were at the convenience of the War Department, for most bridegrooms were officers or enlisted men. Members were limited to one lump of sugar in their coffee. The club emanated a military air—in the parties for sons leaving for service, in the constant swirl of army and navy officers coming and going, in the bridal couples using furloughs for weddings. With rationing, the club instituted meatless days and encouraged members' wives to take streetcars downtown on theater nights. With plants operating seven days a week, the DAC began doing brisk weekend business.

The city's first freeways, the Davison and Willow Run (I-94), took workers to factory jobs. In June 1943, Ford Motor Company's Willow Run plant had 42,331 workers building 650 planes per month.

Abroad, there were still numerous battles to be fought, but optimism was in the air.

Body by Fisher, a division of General Motors, summed up Detroit's role in the winter of 1944 in a full-page ad in the *DAC News*: "The men who do the fighting whether on land, sea or in the air know how important it is to have the best equipment. They realize the work we do in factories can, if done well enough, give them a combat advantage." In the tag line, an X crossed out the word "Body" and replaced it with "Armament." It was a mindset played out in factories all over town. Detroit was the Arsenal of Democracy.

At the club, bandleader Jean Goldkette returned to where he had begun his meteoric rise twenty-five years earlier to entertain crowds with his big band dance music. Some 260 men had been elected to resident membership, and more than 50 nonresidents joined in 1943.

One of America's foremost industrialists, Marvin Coyle, was the new club president, inheriting from outgoing leader Carl Breer "a period of changing conditions and sometimes perplexing problems, unusual opportunities and accomplishments."

Rationing and a forty-eight-hour workweek netted unforeseen profits in 1943 for the DAC. For the first half of 1944, the club saw a net profit of $68,470. While leaders hoped to complete renovation of the kitchens and installation of new equipment, a materials shortage stalled the plan. Still, work progressed on changes to the bowling alley, and a study was conducted to determine the cost of remodeling guest rooms. "A depleted staff worked extremely hard in an all out effort to keep the club up to standards," Coyle reported. "The club never bought or served anything it didn't have a perfect right to have under the strictest interpretation of OPA regulations."

The Office of Price Administration (OPA) was created by FDR to stabilize price controls and had power to ration scarce supplies, including sugar, coffee, meats and processed foods. An emergency effort to protect the club's dwindling liquor supply was taken by the directors—no Scotch whiskey would be served in any private dining room and no rationed liquor to private parties unless all the guests were members. Volume in the cigar department suffered through an inability to get adequate supply. Frequently, the club ran out of the top four brands of cigarettes. Meat rations were cut 40 percent. Ice cream was also less in evidence around the clubhouse.

The first DAC Father-Daughter Party was staged in June 1944 and proved to be one of the most popular affairs in club history. The only regrettable aspect of this super glamorous party was that every dad and daughter who wanted to attend couldn't be accommodated. The annual party is still a beloved tradition, as is the Father-Son Party that began in 1925.

Charlie Hughes sent a verbal bouquet to industrial leaders in July for their unsung war production efforts. These automotive leaders, many members of the DAC, had been hard at work for years to meet military demands. "The Sloans, Kellers, Coyles, Fords, Kaisers, Klinglers and all the rest are not

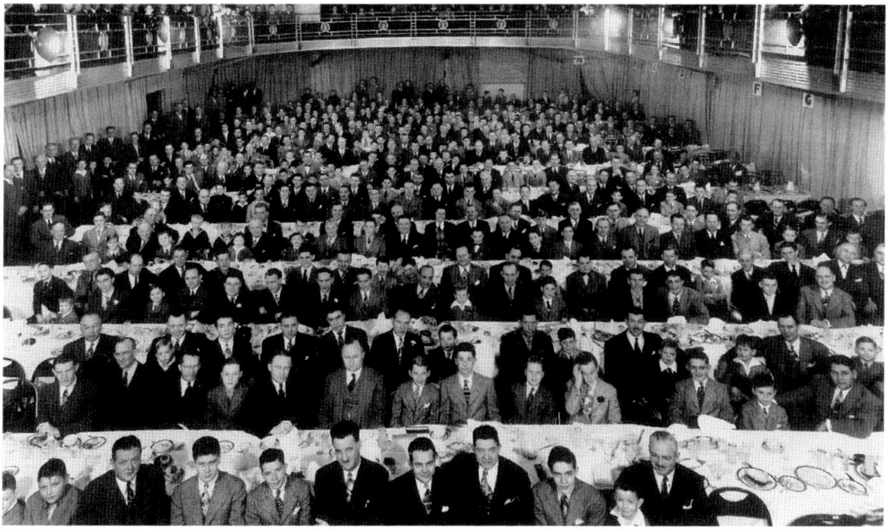

A DAC Father-Son Party in the late 1940s. *DAC archives.*

going to get an extra star on their uniforms for the unbelievable jobs they've done but they should," Hughes opined. "The public has no conception of the miracles they've accomplished."

Senior club member Jim Schroth still has a framed proclamation from the War Production Board given to his stepfather, longtime DAC member C. Ray Davisson, in honor of his service. The late Davisson, a longtime club bowler and president of the Brooker Electric Co., was director of the plumbing and heating division of the War Production Board.

Women of the DAC were engaged in various volunteer projects for the war effort, too. Mrs. Fred Zeder Jr., a nurse's aid, worked in the local Red Cross nurse recruitment office. Assisting with the annual War Chest campaign was Mrs. Jean deKuyper, who also sat on the board of the Naval Recreation Center. Both were wives of DAC members in active military service.

In those historic times, the DAC was in the best condition ever, President Coyle, a GM executive, told members in his annual report. The club made an appeal to members in September 1944 to donate fishing gear for U.S. Marines recovering from malaria in Oregon.

The DAC marked its first and only casualty of war in September 1944 in the loss of twenty-three-year-old junior member PFC Jack Bolton, USMC, killed in the attack on Peleliu Island in the South Pacific, where the marines saw some of their fiercest fighting. Before serving his country, Bolton was almost a daily fixture at the club and the nephew of 1940 DAC president Martin Callahan.

Many DAC members served in all branches of the military during the war; 216 names were listed in a service honor roll in the 1944 roster. That December, the club sent a beautifully crafted Christmas card to all its members in the armed forces.

By 1945, the club found it increasingly difficult to stage big events, with rationing leading to shortages of food, liquor and tobacco. A scarcity of hired help and the inability to get building materials to carry out remodeling projects were also roadblocks. Despite that, by mid-year, the DAC had earned an operating profit of almost $26,000. To offset the effect of the shortages, private parties with less than 80 percent members in attendance were abolished.

The club celebrated its thirtieth anniversary in April 1945 by hosting nine hundred wounded soldiers from the Percy Jones Army Hospital at Fort Custer, Battle Creek, the largest medical installation operated by the army. The veterans were assembled in groups of three hundred and bussed to Detroit. They saw a Tigers baseball game and enjoyed cocktails, lobster and a floor

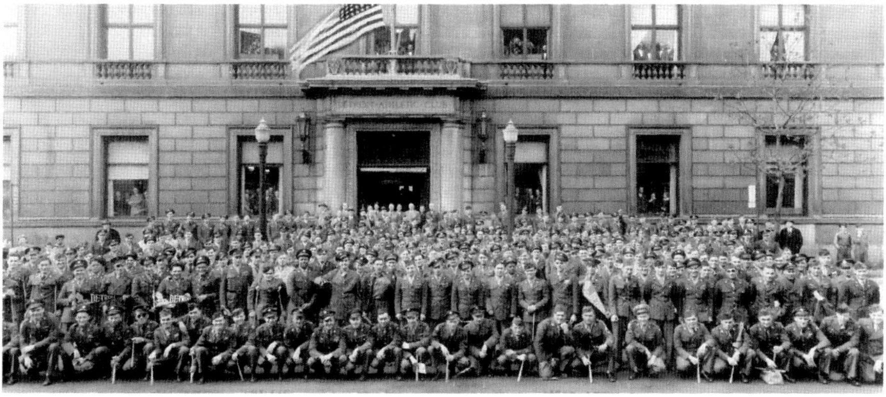

The DAC honored wounded veterans at the clubhouse in April 1945. *DAC archives.*

show. Eighty well-coifed young women, daughters of DAC members, danced with the veterans before a police escort returned the heroes to Battle Creek.

Before V-J Day, the food situation had become critical. Club manager Walter S. Cummings caught a lucky break when he heard of a train derailment in Dearborn and was able to procure 2,100 pounds of chicken bound for New York, stocking the club's huge refrigerators.

V-J Day elicited happy noise and celebration on Madison Avenue. The following day, jubilant diners filled the Main Dining Room to capacity.

With members of the armed forces coming home, the club saw three or four new members return each month to the bowling alleys, squash courts and dining rooms, anxious to resume civilian life. By the time the war ended, the membership had a waiting list of 500 names, certainly for many with no chance of being elected. From a wartime peak of 220 army and navy members, those numbers dwindled by 20 per month. Not surprisingly, these members were mostly affiliated with the armed forces production ordnance division.

After thirty-two long and difficult months of rationing, by late 1945 club members could savor a thick, juicy steak, crisp bacon and sweet crepe suzettes. It would be a much longer wait for quality Scotch whiskey to flow again.

An invitation to members for the annual New Year's Eve party to welcome 1946 promised "a delightful open house affair. The worst of all wars is over."

Following the Allied victory, Knudsen resigned his commission as general and returned to Detroit to a hero's welcome. Flag-waving celebrants lined Woodward Avenue for a parade to honor the man who had helped transform

Detroit into a military production center. A dinner at the Masonic temple drew five thousand well-wishers, including Michigan governor Harry Kelly and U.S. Army general George Marshall.

While Knudsen returned to GM as a member of the board, he was past the mandatory retirement age of sixty-five and, to his regret, ceased active company involvement. Knudsen was presented with numerous honors, including the Distinguished Service Medal and a Gold Cross presented by the king of Denmark. He died on April 27, 1948, after a series of strokes.

With their military mission accomplished, the automotive companies of Detroit returned to domestic vehicle production, closing a shining chapter as America's "Arsenal of Democracy."

Chapter 17

FAMOUS GUESTS AND VISITORS

If the walls of the DAC Clubhouse could talk, what a lively story they'd tell. For as long as the club has existed, it has attracted famous members and visitors, including presidents, royalty, politicians, war heroes, top athletes and A-list entertainers.

Numerous automotive icons had membership. Henry Ford enjoyed a regular clip in the barber's chair and a quiet lunch. The Dodge brothers, Horace and John, threw lavish parties. One soiree had the pool area transformed into a Venetian setting, complete with bobbing gondolas. Another saw the ladies' dining room decorated as a Hawaiian paradise.

World-famous golfer Walter Hagen for years called a sixth-floor suite home, making occasional midnight raids on the club's kitchen and hosting cocktail parties for friends on the pool deck.

Today, NBA hall-of-famer and Detroit mayor Dave Bing is a member, often seen going into meetings and club events. Tony Award–winning actress Elaine Stritch, Academy Award winner George Clooney, Italian tenor Andrea Bocelli and crooner Harry Connick Jr. are all more recent guests.

In 1916, Woodrow Wilson was the first sitting president to visit the DAC, in town to address the inaugural World's Salesmanship Congress. A panoramic photograph of Wilson amid a throng of delegates outside the clubhouse is now displayed in the Abbey. Wilson reportedly shook five thousand hands in front of the DAC cigar counter while Mrs. Wilson rested in the Palm Room attended by a Secret Service officer.

Sporting a walrus mustache, Teddy Roosevelt also visited in 1916, admiring the club's fine Carl Akeley elephant sculpture. Other visitors of that era were Marshall Ferdinand Foch, Allied commander of the Western

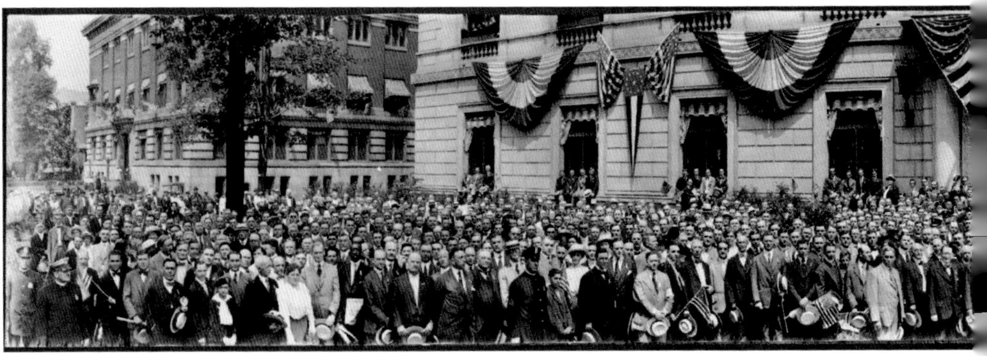

Front in 1918, and General John J. "Black Jack" Pershing, commander of the American Expeditionary Forces.

In more recent times, President George H.W. Bush and later Vice President Al Gore shook hands with Executive Club Manager J.G. Ted Gillary. In 2000, presidential hopefuls George W. Bush and Al Gore visited the club. Later, Secretary of State Condoleezza Rice took a breakfast meeting there with newspaper editors.

In the early years, a captivated audience heard the great magician Harry Houdini give a lecture on spiritualism—one that prompted a letter to the editor of the *DAC News* from Sir Arthur Conan Doyle, a rabid non-believer. Aviation pioneer Amelia Earhart and globetrotting journalist Lowell Thomas also drew crowds to their DAC forums.

World War I flying ace Eddie Rickenbacker was the club's first honorary member. Later, the University of Michigan's first football coach, Fielding Yost, and aviator Charles Lindbergh were so honored. In 1932, the great British statesman Sir Winston Churchill took an overnight room while in Detroit for a lecture.

Live entertainment at the DAC was on par with shows at the top hotels in New York. The inimitable George M. Cohan, Will Rogers, Bob Hope, Bing Crosby, Fanny Brice and Victor Borge entertained in floor shows. So did Edgar Bergen and his wooden sidekick, Charlie McCarthy; George Gobel; Gordon and Sheila MacRae; and pianist Roger Williams. John Philip Sousa and his three-hundred-piece band and Jean Goldkette with his trailblazing jazz orchestra had DAC members dancing.

Olympic swimmer and *Tarzan* star Johnny Weissmuller claimed the world record for the 220-yard freestyle in the club pool. Decades later, a "pool shark" of a different stripe, billiards hustler Minnesota Fats, put on an exhibition at the club in 1964.

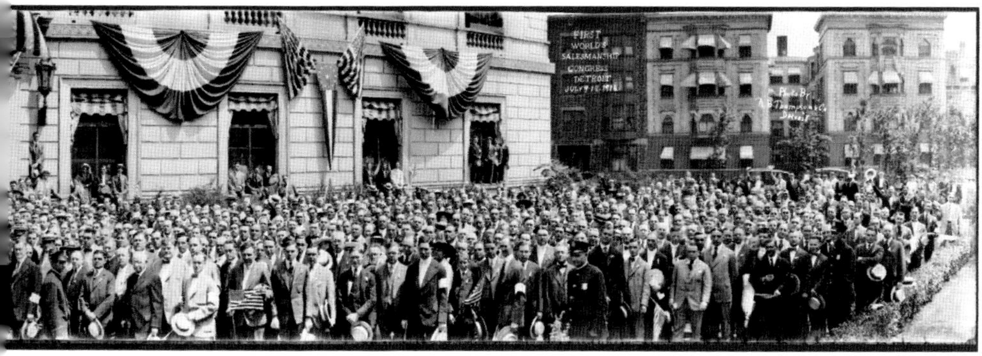

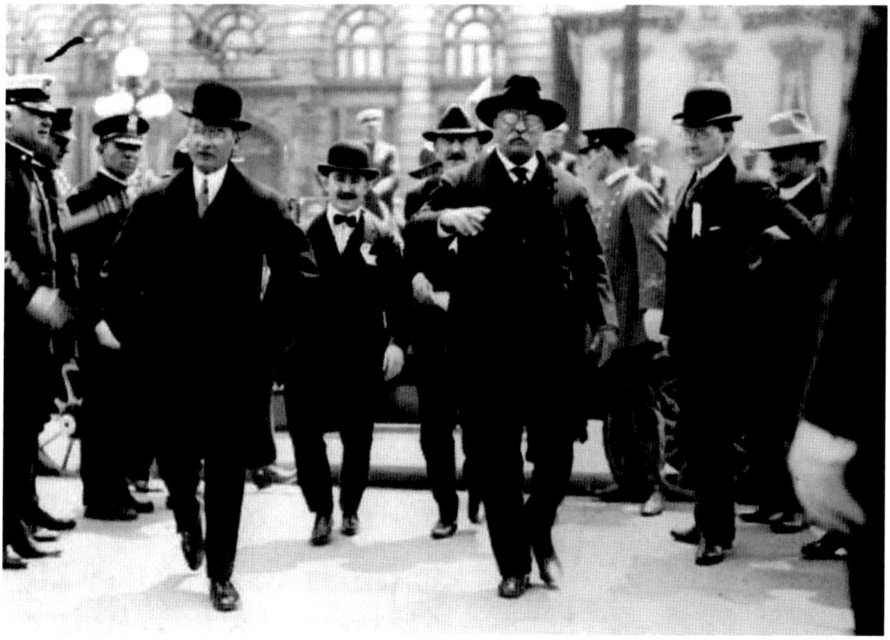

Above: Teddy Roosevelt with Hugh Chalmers (left) enters the DAC in 1916. DAC News *archives.*

Top panoramic: President Woodrow Wilson, flanked by Henry Ford and others at the DAC for the first world's salesmanship conference in July 1916. *DAC archives.*

Edward Albert, prince of Wales and later the duke of Windsor, was given an overnight room with a shower but confessed he didn't like "those sprays" and was accommodated in the Turkish bath. The prince also enjoyed a lesson in cocktail mixing in a private suite during his Prohibition-era visit.

Sportswriter Grantland Rice, humorist Robert Benchley and newspaper columnist Ed Sullivan also appeared. Advice columnist Ann Landers, the first female speaker for the Beavers popular luncheon series, attracted a full house. Numerous sports headliners addressed the Beavers, including Pete Rose, Arnold Palmer and arch rival coaches Bo Schembechler and Woody Hayes.

Military and industrial leaders often visited during Word War II, as did entertainers on USO tours. One day, the Main Dining Room featured a table at lunch with Groucho Marx, Bert Lahr, Jimmy Cagney and Olivia De Havilland.

Dinah Shore belted out tunes for DAC audiences in the 1950s, as did Robert Goulet. Bandleader Lawrence Welk, Flo Ziegfeld and his follies and W.C. Fields charmed earlier club audiences.

World-renowned economist Milton Friedman learned that he had won the Nobel Prize when he arrived at the club in 1979 for a routine event and was met by a swarm of journalists.

It was in the main lobby that a staff member confronted filmmaker Michael Moore on his 1989 quest to find then GM chairman Roger Smith for the documentary film *Roger and Me*.

Michael Jordan and Roger Staubach visited during Super Bowl XL in 2006. Detroit host city festivities fell under the direction of club member Roger Penske, business mogul and record-holding Indy 500 race team owner.

Former mayors and Michigan governors, including George Romney, have been active members. In their tenure, Governors Jennifer Granholm and now Rick Snyder are familiar faces. Auto czars, chief economists, top bankers and builders converge regularly in clubhouse gatherings.

The "Queen of Soul," Aretha Franklin, hosted her 2011 Christmas party for family and friends at the DAC, joining the Four Tops in a moving rendition of "Silent Night."

Chapter 18

GROWTH AND TURBULENCE MARK MID-CENTURY

After the sacrifices of the Great Depression and World War II, DAC members began enjoying a better life in the 1950s, thanks to a prolonged period of growth and increased wealth not seen since the Roaring Twenties. By the time the club celebrated its fiftieth anniversary in 1965, the auto industry was enjoying unprecedented growth, yet the decade was rocked by turbulence ranging from race riots to political assassinations.

But before the turmoil of the 1960s came the robust growth of the booming 1950s. Club members were chosen for top administrative posts in the Eisenhower administration. General Motors president and DAC member Harlow Curtis was *Time* magazine's Man of the Year in 1955 as the automaker became the first corporation in the world to generate over $1 billion in net profits.

The DAC itself was featured in the news. In a flattering profile published in January 1955 in *Holiday*, a national travel magazine, the writer described a thriving prestigious club with floor shows featuring "the same entertainers as seen at the Plaza and Waldorf Astoria in New York." *Sports Illustrated* covered the rivalry between DAC bowlers and athletic clubs from Buffalo, Cleveland and Pittsburgh.

The "Big Three" automakers, GM, Ford and Chrysler, were funding $2 billion in expansion projects by 1955, and Detroit's rising civic center was taking shape at the foot of Woodward Avenue with construction of the Veteran's Memorial, Ford Auditorium and City County buildings.

Club members in top government posts included Eisenhower's defense secretary, Charles Wilson, a former GM president; Postmaster General

Arthur Summerfield; and budget director Joseph Dodge, responsible for the control of more money than any administration prior.

Although it became America's fifth-largest city in 1953 with a population of 1.84 million, Detroit would lose almost 200,000 residents by 1960. Crime rose as unemployment spiked by the end of the decade as the Packard and Studebaker car companies went bust. Factories shed jobs with the increased use of automation.

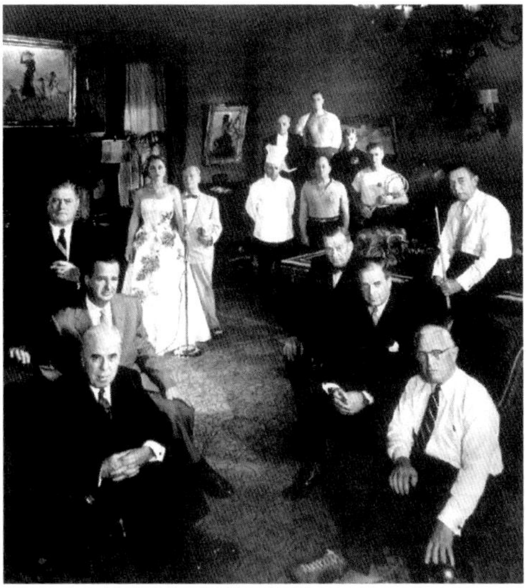

This photo appeared in *Holiday* magazine in 1954 with a story about famous DAC members. Benson Ford is seated second from left, and Indy 500 two-time winner Tommy Milton is seated third from right. DAC News *archives,* Holiday *magazine image.*

Still, consumers were spending freely. Auto sales surged to 5.5 million by the mid-1950s, and a growing number of households added a second car. Buyers snapped up appliances like washers, dryers, refrigerators and television sets.

The city's demographics changed as many residents moved to the suburbs. An influx of African Americans from the South—from 300,000 in 1950 to 482,000 a decade later—came for work in the factories.

With the outbreak of the Korean War, defense contracts poured into the Motor City, but automotive production was not halted, nor was there widespread rationing like in World War II.

There was a passing of the club's old guard, starting with the retirement of longtime manager Walter Cummings in 1950, at the age of seventy. Notable longtime members passed away, including former mayor and thirty-year Detroit city councilman John C. Lodge, Detroit Tigers owner Walter O. Briggs, journalist and author Malcolm Bingay and longtime club secretary and *DAC News* founder and publisher Charles Hughes. To memorialize Hughes's years of service, honorary member Frederick C. Matthaei commissioned New York sculptor Jane Wasey to create a bronze bust of Hughes. The club was presented with the bronze as an anonymous gift in 1954. Nearly sixty years later, it's displayed in the sixth-floor Hughes Chalmers Board Room.

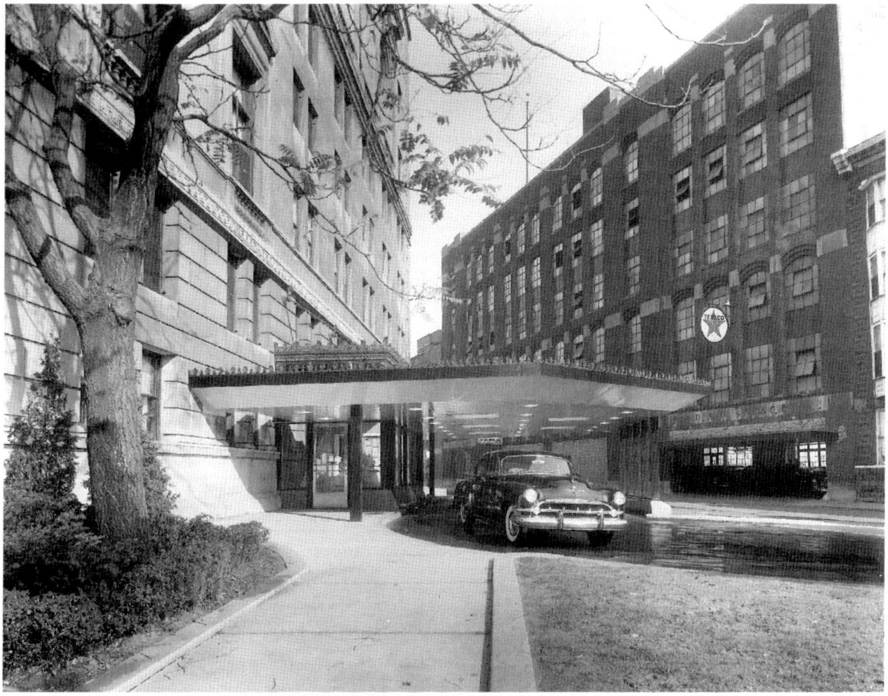

The Randolph entrance in the 1950s. *DAC archives.*

Two other important works of art came into the club in the 1950s: the bronze figure *Dicobolus* (the discus thrower), a gift of the estate of DAC member Hugo J. Hesse; and a copy of George Healy's portrait of Abraham Lincoln by Adrian Lamb, commissioned to counterbalance the club's George Washington portrait.

The club finalized its single biggest acquisition since 1915 when it made a deal with the Gray family estate to buy the old DAC garage across Randolph Street for $407,200.

In 1959, the senior membership classification was added and included all resident and non-resident members who had been with the club for at least thirty years. Initially, 164 members were eligible.

Even before the devastating race riots of 1967, Detroit's population was dropping. By 1960, the city counted 1.67 million residents, about the same number as in 1940.

The long-anticipated $70 million Cobo Hall and Convention Center opened and hosted its first auto show in 1960. Nationwide that year, domestic car sales returned to 6.5 million units, but foreign producers were cutting in, controlling 6.5 percent of the market share.

With the 1960 Summer Olympics in Melbourne, DAC athletic director Clarence Pinkston, an Olympic gold medalist four decades earlier, was instrumental in bringing the U.S. swim team trials to the Motor City. Pinkston had trained DAC member Clarke Scholes, who took gold in the one-hundred-meter freestyle at the 1952 Olympics in Helsinki. He had also groomed champion swimmer and future club president Bill Prew, whose Olympic ambitions were dashed in 1940 by World War II. Just short of thirty-five years as athletic director, Pinkston died in November 1961. The club found another former Olympic swimming champ in Rex Aubrey, a native Australian who had set a world record for one hundred yards at Yale.

The club's fiftieth-anniversary celebration in 1965 under President Frank Kenney, one of Detroit's best-known attorneys, included an Easter Sunday reception attended by nearly two thousand members and wives. Dominating the lobby for the party was a three-thousand-pound cake that stood fifteen feet high, decorated with thousands of sugar spun roses. The *DAC News* published a hardcover golden anniversary history book to mark the occasion.

That same year, a new membership category, the Intermediates, was created for young members. There had been "juniors" since 1915, but they were only sons of members.

The club expanded its base with the purchase of the Cross Street property behind the clubhouse and tore down two old apartment buildings for much-needed parking. Among a litany of renovations throughout the 1960s, the gym was refurbished to make it more multipurpose-friendly and the accounting department received its first computer.

The defining event of the decade began early on Sunday morning, July 23, 1967, when Detroit police raided an illegal after-hours club, or "blind pig," on the corner of Twelfth Street and Clairmount on the near Westside. Confrontations between police and on-lookers escalated into one of the most destructive race riots in U.S. history. Before it was over nearly a week later, forty-three people were dead, hundreds were injured, more than seven thousand were arrested and five thousand were left homeless from nearly two thousand fires set around the city. The Michigan National Guard and U.S. Army troops helped restore order.

There is little historical record of what occurred in the clubhouse that week, just six miles from the spot where the rioting erupted. Printing of the August issue of the *DAC News* was delayed due to "the civil anarchy," and the magazine carried a photo of club member Mike Kuckelman in his National Guard uniform armed with a rifle guarding an entrance to Hudson's downtown store.

By August, Michigan governor George Romney and Detroit mayor Jerome P. Cavanagh had asked DAC member Joseph L. Hudson Jr., chairman of the Hudson's department store chain, to head a "New Detroit" Committee. Other club members on the board included GM chairman James Roche, Henry Ford II, Chrysler chairman Lynn Townsend, Detroit Edison's Walker Cisler and Michigan Bell president William Day. The committee's work led to the creation of New Detroit, Inc., a nonprofit organization blending business, civic, grass-roots and religious groups together to address social ills.

Also moved to action by the devastating riots, Detroit homemaker Eleanor Josaitis, who joined the DAC in 1998 and remained a member until her death in 2011, teamed with the Reverend William Cunningham to found Focus: HOPE.

The decade ended with another hopeful sign as the Economic Development Corporation of Greater Detroit was founded to foster the growth of African American–owned businesses.

Lynn Townsend became DAC president in 1969, the first automotive executive to hold that office in seven years. Besides being a member of New Detroit, in 1970, Townsend was named by President Nixon to chair the National Alliance of Businessmen, a joint effort with the U.S. Department of Labor to hire and train disadvantaged jobless persons.

Meanwhile Detroit's automotive factories were still working to meet the demand for bigger cars with thirstier engines, with little sign of inflation or rising gas prices to come.

Chapter 19

COMMITMENT TO DETROIT AND DIVERSITY

With residents leaving Detroit in droves after the 1967 riots and downtown businesses succumbing to the lure of new skyscrapers in the suburbs, leaders of the Detroit Athletic Club grappled with the idea of joining the mass exodus of the 1970s. Yet for all the valid reasons to leave—urban decay, a rise in crime, rampant inflation—DAC leadership, after careful consideration, opted to stay in the irreplaceable downtown clubhouse designed by Albert Kahn in 1915. By the 1980s, the DAC would become a more diverse club, with minorities and women admitted to full voting membership.

Unlike other cities like New York or Chicago, Detroit's investment community had not financed new projects. The club and the downtown core suffered from a growing malaise. It was partially thanks to traditional groups like the Beavers, the Bowlers and the Blackballers that the DAC kept going through the difficult 1970s.

Dwight Havens, a DAC member who was president of the Greater Detroit Chamber of Commerce in 1970, took the city's leadership to task for not doing enough to improve its plight. Responding to the charge of indifference, the business community created Detroit Renaissance, a committee of top public- and private-sector leaders dedicated to bringing about an economic resurgence. Funded primarily by the Big Three automakers, the committee was led by co-chairmen Henry Ford II, a third-generation DAC member, and Max Fisher, who joined the club years later. Numerous club members served on Detroit Renaissance, including the 1959 and 1961 DAC presidents,

Walker Cisler and Raymond Perring, as well as Thomas Adams, Virgil Boyd, H.B. Cunningham, John Dodds, Hans Gehrke, Joseph Hudson Jr., Fred Matthaei Jr., Roland Mewhort, James Roche and Ken Whalen.

In 1974, club president Fred Colombo stated emphatically that the DAC would remain in the heart of Detroit. In the crowd to hear that speech was Richard Gerstenberg, then board chairman of General Motors, who lauded Colombo's stand. Later, he told a Beavers luncheon crowd that GM also planned to keep its headquarters in the Motor City.

Finally, in the summer of 1977, the massive series of cone-shaped towers on the riverfront offering a luxury hotel, restaurants, offices and retail shops opened to the public. Auto czar Henry Ford II described the gleaming new Renaissance Center as a catalyst for further development and a stabilizing factor for downtown.

A DAC culinary team, led by Chef Daniel Hugelier, took four first-place finishes in the annual Culinary Salon in Chicago in May 1978. Hugelier later captured a rare gold medal in the Pan-American Culinary Olympics in New Orleans.

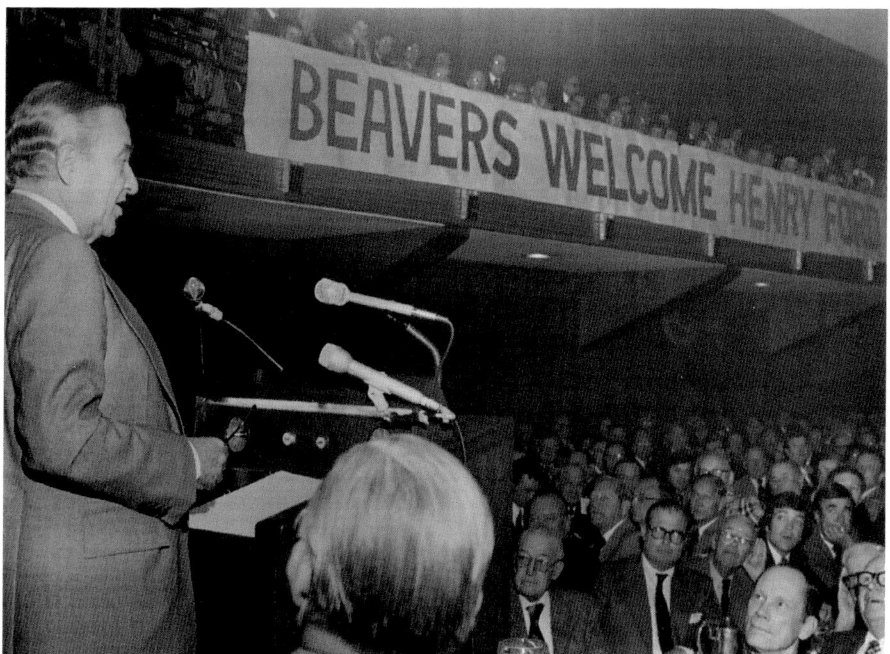

Henry Ford II drew a massive crowd to the Beavers to talk about the new Renaissance Center. *DAC archives.*

As the decade came to a close, the stodgy conservative aura that the DAC projected to outsiders was slowly crumbling. In May 1979, the DAC quietly admitted its first African American member, twenty-seven-year-old Dickinson Wright attorney Robert Young, now a state Supreme Court justice. Soon, other African American men were joining the ranks.

But it took a very public battle, including bad publicity and economic sanctions, before women were admitted as full members. Knowing that the elite DAC was the place for networking, businesswomen (and many club members) supported opening the doors fully. Not all club members agreed.

Double-digit inflation and Detroit's plummeting economy were causes of concern in the early 1980s. In August 1983, the DAC board amended rules to allow spouses of members and female guests to occupy the overnight rooms on the upper floors. Of the twenty-four clubs with which the DAC had reciprocal usage agreements, only one other property—in Australia—restricted occupancy to men only. The change ensured a badly needed revenue source, as room occupancy jumped 65 percent by the following year.

Fully a decade earlier, a group of women had stormed the front door to protest the DAC's policy regarding women. The event that ignited the furor happened on October 16, 1975, when Detroit city councilwoman Maryann Mahaffey was redirected to a side entrance when she arrived for a dinner meeting at the clubhouse. Irate, Mahaffey stormed off indignantly.

Rubbing salt into the wound, the DAC membership voted down an amendment to allow women to become full members in January 1986. Banner headlines proclaimed discrimination, editorials chided the club's policy, newspaper columnists exhorted disgust and cartoonists lampooned the DAC. The brouhaha made national headlines.

Into this quagmire, Kowalski Sausage Company CEO Ron Kowalski became official media liaison as the DAC's 1986 president. Two weeks into his term, Kowalski found himself facing popular Detroit morning radio host J.P. McCarthy on WJR-AM 760 to discuss the hot topic.

In March, three groups, including St. Mary's College of Notre Dame, cancelled events scheduled for the DAC due to the controversy. By April, the board had identified thirty-five resignations related to the issue. Soon, officials from several firms, including Detroit Edison, Michigan Bell, Michigan Consolidated Gas and the Burroughs Corporation, stopped paying club dues for their male executives since they couldn't offer the same perk to women.

In July 1986, the Detroit City Council approved an ordinance sponsored by the club's longtime nemesis, Mahaffey, to force the DAC to enroll women.

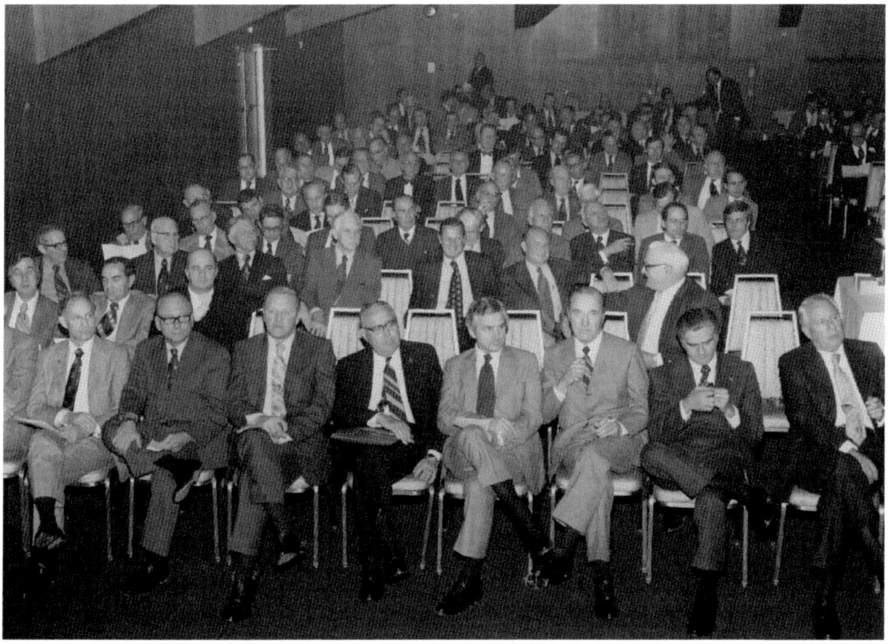

Voting members gather in 1986. DAC News *archives.*

Mayor Coleman A. Young vetoed the measure, saying he wished to avoid litigation, preferring the club make that decision.

In a bizarre theatrical twist, women in face masks dumped three hundred pairs of high-heeled shoes under the DAC canopy before dawn on August 26, with a sign proclaiming "The real heels are within."

Finally bowing to public and private pressures, the DAC board voted to accept women as full voting members on September 16, 1986. While a swarm of potential female members didn't immediately materialize, the measure was good for the club. When the first two women—stockbroker Marie Vanerian and Michigan Bell executive Katherine Carrick—were admitted as resident members in December 1986, so prominent was the issue that both women merited feature stories in the daily newspapers.

In 2003, Mary L. Kramer would become the first female president of the DAC. She was the first woman elected to a board seat two years earlier, although another female member had held a board appointment in the 1990s.

Chapter 20

DRAMATIC RESTORATION REVITALIZES HISTORIC CLUBHOUSE

The leaders of the modern DAC have proven to be as farsighted as their predecessors, overseeing a multimillion-dollar, ten-year restoration that has returned the clubhouse to its early splendor while offering first-class amenities. This unprecedented series of projects has ranged from the subtle work of professional restorers to large-scale bricks and mortar construction.

Launched in 1997 and continuing through 2007, the initial challenge for the DAC was getting membership on board for the task of transforming the beautiful but dated clubhouse to create a modern building where many of the dollars spent would be on intangibles like plumbing and code work.

One of the first orders of business was hiring a new executive manager. The candidate selected in 1994 was J.G. Ted Gillary, who would oversee this transformation from start to finish. Creating a vision for members was a key to the restoration's success. In 1996, Gillary unveiled a plan centered on preserving the club's unique architectural treasures while modernizing its business, sports and dining facilities. He fine-tuned his plan in presentations before the DAC board and committees, gaining encouragement from club presidents John Prost, Douglas Rasmussen and Thomas Quilter.

Downtown also experienced an awakening in the late 1990s. Around the clubhouse in every direction, Detroit was being revitalized in an exhilarating fashion not seen since the Roaring Twenties. Sports meccas Comerica Park and Ford Field were going up. The newly restored Detroit Opera House, home of Michigan Opera Theatre, was drawing rave reviews. The Gem Theatre—relocated to make way for the new ballpark—found a home just east of the DAC. The Music Hall was wowing fans following a major renovation, as was the elegantly restored Fox Theatre. For the first time in ages, downtown had a defined entertainment district, and the DAC was at its epicenter.

Things were on the upswing inside the clubhouse, too. Through the late 1990s, membership continued to surge, with numbers not seen since the mid-1960s.

On November 4, 1997, the board approved a plan called DAC 2000. Later to be known as Phase I through Phase V, this multiyear restoration returned the clubhouse to its magnificent opulence while updating infrastructure and expanding athletic and dining facilities.

With sound financial footing, an unplanned event in 1997 turned into an even greater motivator for restoration. An employee doing routine maintenance uncovered long-forgotten original decorative paintings on the Main Dining Room ceiling. It was a discovery that DAC director and later president Ken Katz, a professional art restorer, likened to finding a Van Gogh in the attic. DAC painter Wayne Woodard was scraping blistered paint from water damage on a major ceiling beam when he unearthed a patch of frescoes long covered by paint. Members were amazed, and the discovery sparked real excitement.

The room had deteriorated dramatically from its original design: chandeliers and wall sconces were removed and not replaced, the stone block design above the paneling was replaced with acoustical tile and the curtains were faded. The first phase also called for renovating the main kitchen, Reading Room, main lobby and guest rooms and upgrading essential services for $8.2 million. The club used $2.5 million in short-term investments and planned to finance the remainder through a line of credit with three banks.

As those first workers toiled under spotlights on large scaffold platforms, members could see something tangible. Restoration of the main lobby ceiling was used as a tool to sell the project.

When Tom Quilter became president in 1998, he helped shape the specifics of an ambitious agenda, and the club closed for six weeks to begin implementation. The shutdown ran from July 13 to September 8 while the main kitchen was overhauled. Members could abide noise and dust generated by other projects, but completely gutting the kitchen pulled the plug on food service.

Ken Katz's firm, Museum and Conservation Services, was hired to unmask the original frescoes on the Main Dining Room ceiling. The Ladies'

Activities Committee played a key role in identifying the paintings and lobbying for restoration. Substantial funds were also diverted from the guest rooms' budget to pay for ceiling restoration. Nearly three hundred paintings by Scottish artist A. Duncan Carse filled the ceiling with depictions of athletes, landscapes, fruit, centaurs, birds and Mayan masks. Minor beams and all borders were covered in stencils. About 60 percent of the artwork was salvaged, and new landscape scenes were prepared to match the original style, with subjects such as Comerica Park, Ford Field and the Renaissance Center, painted by a trio of Ukrainian craftsmen whom Katz hired.

In the main lobby, workers restored the plaster ceiling, carefully removing eight decades of smoke and grime so that brilliant original hues would shine. Woodworkers installing new sprinklers in the main lobby temporarily removed inch-thick solid walnut boards one foot wide by fourteen feet long. They surmised that boards that size installed in 1915 were probably growing trees during the American Revolution.

From mid-July until Labor Day 1998, some three thousand worker-hours were logged in a noisy, hot, dusty, fume-laden environment. In the Main Dining Room, new chandeliers, window treatments and wall sconces were

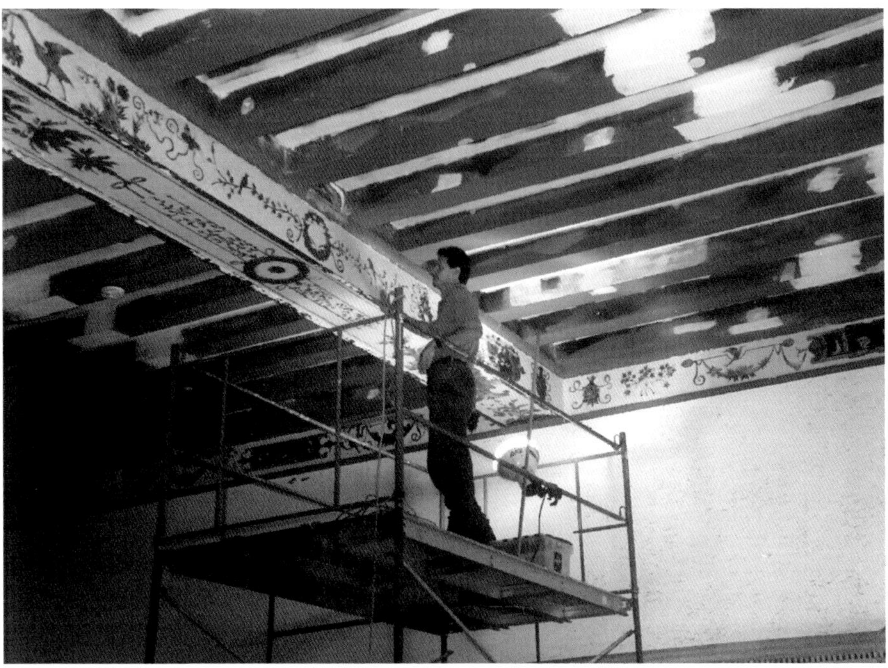

Restorers work on the Main Dining Room ceiling. DAC News *image*.

hung; oak paneling and member entry doors were refinished. Conservators uncovered decorative art and revived Caen stone along the grand staircase and second-floor walls.

The state's oldest architectural firm, the SmithGroup, provided services.

With the exception of that first summer, the club remained open and services were maintained. At times, that required heroic efforts from staff. When the air handling system was powered up for the first time, big puffs of soot permeated furniture, drapes and carpeting in the Grill and Georgian Rooms. Housekeeping crews became experts at last-minute, high-speed cleaning.

As the calendar moved toward the new millennium, a cacophony of hammers, saws and drills roared on a daily basis. Yet weddings, corporate meetings and private parties were held.

In the main lobby, American walnut paneling was stripped, hand-sanded, restained and resealed. Chandeliers and wall sconces were restored, along with the Hauteville marble fireplace. The Madison Avenue revolving door was retooled, while new rugs, window treatments and furniture gave a fresh appearance. Lighting highlighted the ceiling and significant features.

In the Reading Room, workers restored ceiling cornices and ornamental borders and refinished wainscot and the oak parquet floor to frame a new custom rug. Period furniture was restored and the walls recovered. The centerpiece chandelier was entrusted to a restoration specialist, and the four-hundred-pound Edward Caldwell–designed brass, bronze and wood fixture of over one hundred pieces was completely disassembled, cleaned and rewired. Sixteen missing pieces required fabrication of metal replacement castings.

In his five-year improvement plan, Gillary had identified the DAC's guest rooms as the most lucrative profit center in the club. Work was completed to modernize heating and cooling systems, doors and bathrooms, and two disability-compliant rooms were also created.

While the club's public areas sparkled with rediscovered beauty, the lion's share of work occurred behind the scenes, bringing the 1915 clubhouse into the twenty-first century. During Phase II, the Grill Room kitchen and dining areas and Tap Room were a combined project because of the integral nature of infrastructure and service elements. Turning them into modern operations gleaming with historical detail cost $7.8 million.

The Grill's ceiling featured decorative art, but acoustic tiles from an earlier renovation had caused irreparable damage. Conservators identified 150 original colors used by Carse. Construction workers extracted the tiles, the ceiling was re-plastered and decorative painters replicated the original designs. Eighty seats were added for dining, the historic ambiance was refreshed and wine service was enhanced with the creation of a vast, glass-enclosed cellar. In addition to the vaulted ceilings, decorative plaster, woodwork and the tile floors were restored. The original Grill was confined to the area known as "the bricks" covered by tile flooring. Demand led to expansion into the adjacent billiards room, now known as the Grill's carpeted side.

In Phase II, the Grill had to create a new food delivery system to handle increased volume. The kitchen was moved to the former reception area of the main floor court center.

In the Tap Room, the bar was rebuilt in period style and plumbing, lighting and ventilation systems were upgraded. Fire protection, electrical systems and sanitation were updated.

In August 1999, decorative artists took tracings and used them as templates on new plaster. Period furniture was refinished. The Caldwell iron lights in the Grill were refurbished.

As 2000 dawned and Phase III began, resident membership reached capacity (three thousand) with a waiting list, driving up dues to pay for restoration. The sorely needed expansion of the parking garage was essential. In May 2000, construction was begun to add 330 parking spaces for a total of 770, doubling the size of the garage from three to six levels.

Rolled into this phase was a plan to modernize the fourth-floor gymnasium. Walls and ceilings needed fireproofing and code work. Brick that had been covering windows since the late 1980s was removed, and another view of the new ballpark emerged. The beautiful original wood flooring of the oval track was uncovered.

The club commissioned a fresco for the Grill Room depicting the DAC and the downtown skyline, paid for by the newly activated Enrichment Fund. In 2000, the Enrichment Fund and DAC Foundation were created for members to contribute financial support. The foundation supports causes outside the club, like neighborhood beautification and safety. The Enrichment Fund launched the DAC Donors Club as a way for members to fund in-house projects. In the first year, it raised money for restoration of the ceilings in the second-floor hallways.

In February 2001, the DAC Board approved Phase IV, involving the west ends of the third and fourth floors. The major focus was the health and fitness areas. The new women's locker room features three hundred lockers; a revamped wet area with steam, whirlpool, sauna and showers; tanning and

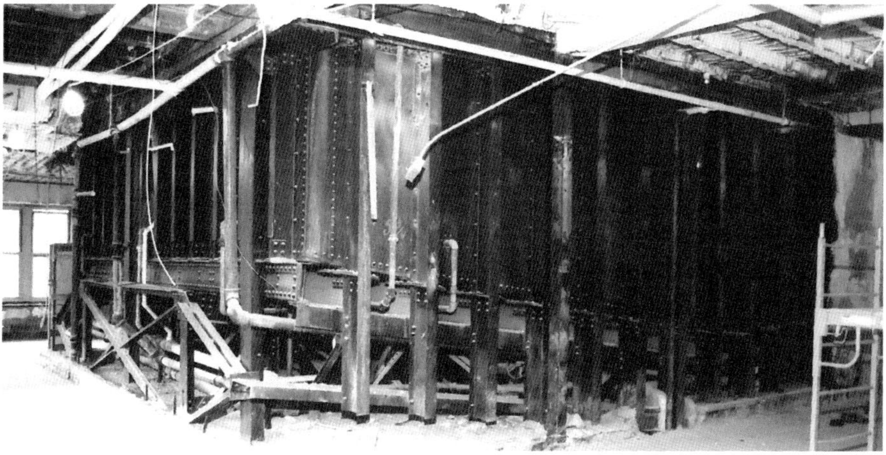

After eighty-plus years, the support structure for the fourth-floor swimming pool was in excellent shape. DAC News *image.*

sleeping rooms; makeup counters; and private dressing rooms. It touts a new private dining area and merchandise counter.

Another third-floor project was expansion of rooms to become Stadium East and West to accommodate larger functions. On the fourth floor, courts were demolished to accommodate an expanded fitness center, with a complete line of aerobic and strength-training equipment, a cardio-entertainment center with multiple televisions, radio and music selections and windows offering sweeping downtown views. Two international squash courts were added to the north side of the fourth floor adjacent to the fitness center.

Outside recognition ranged from the 2001 Special Historic Restoration award from the Detroit Engineering Society to numerous Platinum Club of America awards, voted by an association of professional club members.

Sculptor Samuel Yellin's metal railing along the sweep of the grand staircase was restored in 2003. A team led by Yellin's granddaughter brought the decorative rail back to life by cleaning, re-patinaing, glazing and adding green and reddish tones.

The following year in the Georgian room, artisans re-created the frieze, decorative door pediments and crown molding. Enhanced lighting was installed. Chandeliers and wall sconces were restored and the original glass entry doors re-created.

Spurred by Major League Baseball's All-Star game planned for Comerica Park in 2005 and the National Football League's Super Bowl at Ford Field the

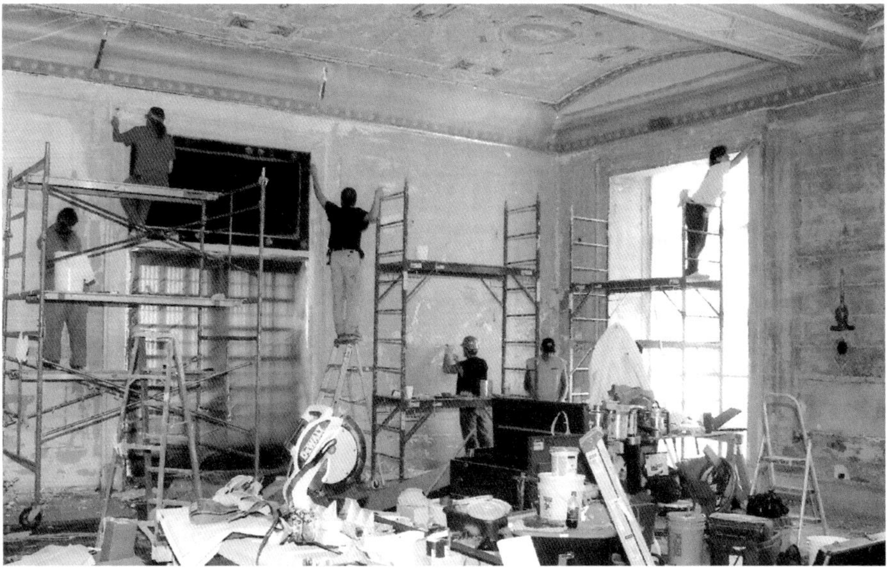

A frenzy of restoration activity in the Pontchartrain Room. DAC News *image.*

following year, the DAC Foundation raised funds to illuminate the clubhouse exterior in time for the games that would put downtown in the spotlight. As the club celebrated its ninetieth anniversary, members stood outside at dusk to see the clubhouse artfully lit for the first time.

The final project phase included restoration of the elegant Pontchartrain Room (once known as the Palm Room). That same year, the club redid the men's locker room (uncovering the original frame of the fourth-floor pool) and restored the Randolph rooms.

No major renovations were completed in 2006–7, but the club invested millions for ongoing improvements, highlighting the fact that the DAC was continuing to enhance its Albert Kahn clubhouse even beyond the various phase projects.

In 2007, the club acquired a large tent for its back lot stadium pavilion to host tailgates; the following year, a high-end restroom was added. Landscape improvements along Madison Avenue, a flag display and third-floor athletic corridor and mezzanine business center upgrades were completed.

Despite economic challenges in Detroit, the DAC has remained financially stable and continued to rack up local and state business awards, including the prestigious Michigan Quality Leadership Award, the first hospitality business so honored in the history of the program.

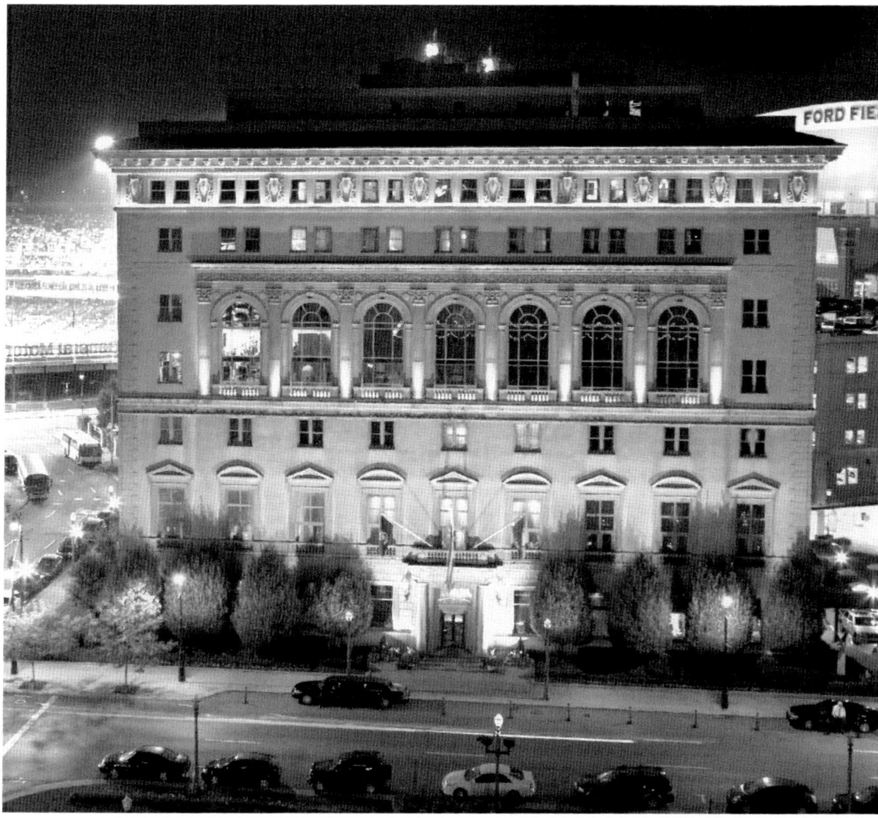

The clubhouse exterior today as the club gets ready to celebrate the building's 100th year in 2015. DAC News *image*.

The phased projects were not an ending to the clubhouse renovations. In 2011, the DAC spent millions remodeling all the guest rooms and creating the new Tranquility Spa, as well as other in-house projects.

Perhaps most fitting among the recent refurbishments was the stunning transformation of a sixth-floor suite into the Hughes Chalmers Board Room. Named for one of the club's most influential founding figures, Charles Hughes, and the DAC's first president, Hugh Chalmers, it is a fitting tribute to a long-enduring institution.

BIBLIOGRAPHY

Books

Bingay, Malcolm W. *Detroit Is My Own Hometown*. New York: Bobbs-Merrill Company, 1946.

Burton, Clarence M., ed.-in-chief, with William Stocking and Gordon K. Miller, assoc. eds. *The City of Detroit, Michigan*. Vols. I–IV. Detroit, MI: S.J. Clarke Publishing Company, 1922.

Davis, Donald Finlay. *Conspicuous Production: Automobiles and Elites in Detroit, 1899–1933*. Philadelphia: Temple University Press, 1933.

Davis, Michael W.R. *Detroit's Wartime Industry, Arsenal of Democracy*. Charleston, SC: Arcadia Publishing, 2007.

Falls, Joe. *The Detroit Tigers, an Illustrated History*. New York: Walker & Company, 1989.

Kimes, Beverly Rae. *Standard Catalog of American Cars 1805–1942*. Iola, WI: Krause Publications, Inc., 1996.

Lodge, John C. *I Remember Detroit*. Detroit, MI: Wayne State University Press, 1949.

Marquis, Albert Nelson, ed. *The Book of Detroiters, 1914*. Chicago: A.N. Marquis & Company, 1914.

Murray, Mike, ed. *Lions Pride: Sixty Years of Detroit Lions Football*. N.p.: Taylor Publishing Company and the Detroit Lions, Inc., 1993.

Poremba, David Lee. *Detroit: City of Champions*. Charleston, SC: Arcadia Publishing, 1998.

Ross, Robert B., and George Catlin. *Landmarks of Detroit: A History of the City*. Detroit, MI: Evening News Association, 1898.

Seltzer, Lawrence H. *A Financial History of the American Automobile Industry*. Boston: Houghton-Mifflin Company, 1928.

Stark, George W. *City of Destiny*. Detroit, MI: Arnold-Powers, Inc., 1943.
Stump, Al. *Cobb: A Biography*. Chapel Hill, NC: Algonquin Books, 1994.
Voyles, Kenneth H., and John A. Bluth. *The Detroit Athletic Club 1887–2001*. Charleston, SC: Arcadia Publishing, 2001.
Woodford, Frank B., and Arthur M. Woodford. *All Our Yesterdays: A Brief History of Detroit*. Detroit, MI: Wayne State University Press, 1969.

Periodicals

Batchelor, Eddie. "Detroit Boat Club Champion Four." *Detroit Saturday Night*, August 12, 1911.
———. "Jake Mazer." *Detroit Saturday Night*, 1930.
Borth, Christy. "The First 50 Years." *DAC News*, April 1965.
DAC News. Special history editions, October 2001 through October 2011.
Day, Jennifer. "Edward A. Batchelor, Sr." *DAC News*, October 1995.
Detroit News. "DAC Gridders of 1896." March 27, 1934.
———. "Detroit's Best Indoor Organization." 1912.
Falls, Joe. "The No. 1 Baseball Writer in America." *Sporting News*, August 28, 1965.
Forbes, Dr. E.B. "Spilling the Pins." *DAC News*, January 1916.
Ford, Malcolm. "Hurdling." *Outing* magazine, July 1891.
———. "Miscellaneous Jumping." *Outing* magazine, June 1892.
Grosse Pointe News. Obituaries, July 25, 1968.
Lodge, John C. "Blazing the DAC Trail." *DAC News*, January 1916.
Manning, John C. "Started in Detroit." *Detroit Free Press*, March 7, 1962.
New York Times. "Amateur League Splits." February 13, 1916.
Outing magazine. "The Dissension in the Athletic World." January 1889.
———. "Sprinters." May 1891.
Russell, John A. "The Detroit Athletic Club." *Outing* magazine. December 1888, 205–16.
University of Pennsylvania Archives (1861–1913). Michael C. Murphy, Penn Biographies

A wide range of additional newspaper clips, stories and items were used throughout the research of all the chapters. Every newspaper in Detroit's long history was used as part of this extensive process. Many of the original clippings come from historic scrapbooks owned by the DAC dating back to the building of the modern clubhouse. These precious scrapbooks are crumbling yet remain a gold mine of information, particularly about the creation of the DAC Clubhouse on Madison Avenue. Other newspaper materials were used through the Detroit Public Library's microfilm collection.

INDEX

D

E

F

G

H

I

J

K

L

M

N

O

P

Q

R

S

T

U

V

W

Y

ABOUT THE AUTHORS

Mary Rodrique is a contributing writer for the *DAC News*. A native Detroiter and a journalism graduate (Phi Beta Kappa) of Wayne State University, she has written numerous magazine and newspaper articles on topics of historic interest. She worked as a newspaper editor and writer for several years before joining the Detroit Athletic Club staff in 2002.

Ken Voyles is editor and publisher of the award-winning *DAC News* magazine, the longest-published monthly magazine in Michigan. A journalism graduate of Wayne State University and native Detroiter, he spent more than twenty-five years in the newspaper business throughout southeast Michigan before joining the DAC in 1999. He is an award-winning writer and photographer. This is his second published work of history.